SCHOLASTIC

CCSS
SUPPORTS THE COMMON CORE STATE STANDARDS

Grades
5 and UP

Independent Reading in the Age of Common Core

Sue Cannone-Calick
&
Elizabeth Henley

New York • Toronto • London • Auckland • Sydney
Mexico City • New Delhi • Hong Kong • Buenos Aires

Teaching Resources

Acknowledgements:

When we started this project, we believed strongly in the power of SmartNotes, but we didn't know where it would lead us. It has taken us through hot summer days, early Saturday mornings, and late afternoons. Along the way, support came from our friends and colleagues at Ardsley Middle School: In particular, Dr. Lauren Allan, from whom we received the encouragement and faith to "get messy," and Edgar McIntosh for opening doors to us. Thank you.

To our families: Thank you. Your excitement, and energy bubbled over into this book.

Thank you again to the community of Ardsley; SmartNotes began with you.

Dedication:

To the students of Ardsley Middle School

Cover design: Jorge J. Namerow
Cover photograph: © Monkeybusinessimages/Big Stock
Interior design: Melinda Belter
Development editor: Joanna Davis-Swing
Editor: Sarah Glasscock
Copy editor: Carol Ghiglieri
ISBN: 978-0-545-44275-6
Copyright © 2013 by Sue Cannone-Calick and Elizabeth Henley
All rights reserved.
Printed in the U.S.A.

1 2 3 4 5 6 7 8 9 10   40   20 19 18 17 16 15 14 13

Contents

Introduction

No matter which subject you're teaching—be it English language arts, science, math, or social studies—teaching reading is your most important job. And, no matter which discipline your students are studying, learning how to be strong readers of content is the focus of the new Common Core State Standards.

Teaching reading is hard; how do we know we are doing it correctly? There is often no immediate, tangible proof. Of course, there are many assessments we can choose from to assess our students' reading. These tools evaluate readers a few times a year and can show growth over time, but they fail to reflect students' everyday learning.

One way to truly gauge students' comprehension is by asking them to share their thinking, either through conversation or writing. In this book, we introduce an effective and efficient tool called SmartNotes that we devised to help students do just that: SmartNotes allow students to share their thinking about a text and gives you valuable information about their comprehension and use of strategies.

The power of SmartNotes is in their simplicity. Students are not intimidated by the process—after all, they require nothing more than a pencil and a notebook! SmartNotes can be used to launch class discussions, individual conferences, paragraph writing, and test preparation. Holding students accountable for thinking while reading complex fiction and nonfiction texts is the essence of a middle school balanced-literacy program—and the heart of the new Common Core State Standards. SmartNotes help you achieve this.

SmartNotes are a written record of student thinking while reading.

Sue's Story: The Beginning of SmartNotes

The rug got pulled out from under me when our district started its slow move toward a balanced-literacy model. Getting to balanced literacy was an emotional climb for me. As a veteran teacher, I was set in my ways: I thought if Hatchet *by Gary Paulsen was a fifth-grade book, then all of my fifth graders, in all of my classes should be able to read it. Then our district brought in a staff developer who told us that all kids were different and posed this question to our group: "Why must every fifth grader read the same book?"*

WHAT! I wanted to scream. This went against everything I had been doing for the last eight years! I felt the sweat beginning to form. I could not answer that simple question. Finally, I offered this feeble attempt at a response: "Because it's a fifth-grade book."

Joanna, the staff developer, kindly and matter-of-factly stated that all fifth graders are not on the same reading level.

How could I not have known this? How could I have assumed that one size fits all when it comes to reading? As this realization hit me, and the more I thought about it, the more overwhelmed I became! How could I throw away eight years of really good lesson plans and start over again? Had I failed my previous students? Then the tears came—really. Change is hard, especially for a veteran teacher with eight years of really good lesson plans!

I started reading about balanced literacy. I found Guiding Readers and Writers *by Irene Fountas and Gay Su Pinnell interesting. I thought Laura Robb's* Teaching Reading in Middle School *was useful, too. I spent a summer reading, but I was still in the same place. How could I use balanced literacy in my middle school class? How could I hold kids accountable for learning during independent reading? How could I measure their growth and understanding during reading? The overwhelmed feeling returned. This is summer vacation, I thought. I'm not supposed to be overwhelmed!*

I wrestled with these questions all summer, and before I knew it, September had rolled around. We had a few more sessions with Joanna, and as a result, I did more thinking, and as a result, I was even more overwhelmed!! I wanted to have the shared experience of reading the core book with students, and I was committed to independent reading. Again, the same questions nagged at me. I needed to make some changes!

During another of our staff development sessions Joanna asked our group, "What are your goals for students as they read?"

Again, I was confounded by a simple question, but I sat quietly and thought and thought. This time, sweat did not form, and I confidently answered, "I want kids to be able to think smartly through a text." For the first time in a while, I was thinking clearly about my reading program, and I had a goal: Smart thinking for all kids! With confidence I set out to achieve my goal.

I tackled my original questions again:

How can I use balanced literacy in my middle school class?

How can I hold kids accountable for learning during independent reading?

How can I measure growth and understanding when reading?

I needed to <u>see</u> smart thinking, so I thought, "Why don't I write down on chart paper what smart thinking looks like?" I envisioned students writing down their thinking. They would record their thoughts as they moved through a book. The kids could see how to think through a book, and I could see and measure their thoughts. This was it! We would write down our smart thinking as we read. Students would write down their thinking on "SmartNotes"!

I was excited. I now had a focus. Balanced literacy could work for middle school students, and balanced literacy could work for me. The shift to balanced literacy meant a commitment to independent reading and self-selection of books. Along with Betsy, my new co-teacher and the school's literacy specialist, I believed that our students needed to do more. We believed that middle school teachers had a responsibility to help students think smartly through a text. This thinking comes in many shapes and sizes. SmartNotes would be the evidence of this thinking. SmartNotes would hold students accountable for their thinking while they read and provide me with data that they were really reading and working. As students read books at their level and wrote SmartNotes, I felt like I had a handle on their comprehension. Active reading meant thinking and writing about text.

About This Book

Using SmartNotes as outlined in this book will help you use independent reading in your Common Core curriculum to enhance student thinking and writing about reading. We discuss the structure of SmartNotes and include sample mini-lessons to show SmartNotes in action across a variety of strategies. A chart on pages 118–128 lists the Common Core State Standards that each sample mini-lesson addresses.

10/27/09 <u>Mixed up Files</u>

• I have a question if any problems are going to happen to them because so far, everything is going great.

• I can infer that Jamie is clever & street-smart because on pg. 46, "Jamie smiled and nodded. 'Mother always says I came from Heaven.' He bowed politely and walked out."

• I can infer that Claudia is hungry for knowledge because on pg. 47, "Claudia informed Jamie that they should take advantage of the wonderful oppurtunity to learn and to study. No other children in all the world since the world began had such an oppurtunity."

This Smart Note shows a student's thinking while reading From the Mixed-Up Files of Mrs. Basil E. Frankweiler.

CHAPTER ONE

Common Core State Standards & Independent Reading

The teaching of reading differs from state to state, county to county, and also teacher to teacher, but in order for students to grow as readers, independent reading must be part of the literacy program. In the past, as teachers embraced fiction—including historical fiction and fantasy—informational texts were often overlooked: unappealing covers, outdated information, and inaccessible formats formerly branded nonfiction texts as too hard and boring, leaving both teachers and students unenthused. When standardized tests began to show a weakness in students' comprehension of nonfiction, states began to update their standards to address this discrepancy. Today, most states have adopted the Common Core State Standards (CCSS), which are brimming with nonfiction reading and writing requirements.

The CCSS require students to be more analytical, metacognitive, and inferential. Students need to know what happens in a text and why authors make certain choices. These standards challenge readers to dig deeply into a text and to support their thinking and writing about reading. Students are expected to tackle complex text independently.

Central to the mission of developing thoughtful readers is independent reading. Carving out at least 15–20 minutes a day devoted to independent reading is essential. Allowing and encouraging middle schoolers to self-select texts that interest them will invest them in reading. They'll be in greater control of their choices—giving them the independence they crave and need. Though it may seem obvious, it is also true: when reading books of their own choosing, readers read more. And all readers improve when they read more.

Establishing Independent Reading Time

Balanced literacy allows teachers to meet learners at their own level. The range of readers in a classroom can be wide: a class of 28 might be reading at 14 different levels. In our classroom, shifting from a traditional—at the front of the room teaching—to a balanced-literacy model required a shift in our roles. We were no longer in charge of students' thinking; we needed to let go, release responsibility, and allow and encourage independence.

In the paradigm of the balanced-literacy model, the teaching of literacy (our focus is on reading) incorporates whole-group, small-group, and independent instruction. Within each mode, teachers have choices about the intensity of their teaching. Balanced literacy, and the thinking behind it, encourages a move away from teacher-directed lessons to student-focused instruction through a workshop model.

In a traditional balanced-literacy classroom, the only sound you'd expect to hear are pages turning and/or whispered conversations, but we realized we needed to hear another sound: the sound of writing. The scratch of pencils on paper is the sound of thinking, and that's why we created SmartNotes, an approach in which students record their thinking as they read independently.

The Workshop Model

Workshop classrooms are successful because each student is moved forward as an individual learner. Workshop classrooms are alive. No day is the same as the day before. Your lesson plan book may look similar to last year's, but your teaching is now dependent on whom you have in front of you. This changes from year to year and class to class.

The following three modes of instruction form the frame for the reading block.

- **Whole-class work:** This work is intended to meet the needs of the bulk of your class. In this component, a mini-lesson should target a specific goal. Goals are determined by your curriculum and the needs of your students. After you model reading strategies, students practice them independently, using their independent reading book.

- **Small-group work:** For some students, the mini-lesson hits home and is internalized. For others, a quick reminder/check-in is sufficient. Still for others, small-group instruction is required.

- **One-to-one conference:** Sitting beside a student and listening to him or her read and learning about his or her thinking is valuable. Having individual conferences allows a teacher to know the reader and teach the specific skill that each student needs. Additionally, it allows you to push a student to think differently—more deeply.

Learning how to understand and talk and write about texts in a deep and thoughtful way is essential for our students. The hybridization of the workshop model and traditional literature study is an effective way to instruct middle school learners. Traditional middle school curriculum is based on literature study, which is similar to the high school approach, so middle schools have to prepare kids for this future. Many teachers at this level, therefore, consider themselves to be teachers of literature rather than teachers of reading. In many middle schools, there is one core text that all students read. The teacher models text analysis through this reading experience, but reading strategies are often not considered. Also not considered are student reading levels or interests. As a result, many students do not fully understand this core text. But text analysis is important. It's necessary for students to grow, so reading-strategy instruction should not be ignored. Students at the middle school level still need direct instruction in how to be strong readers.

SETTING UP A STRUCTURE AND ROUTINES

Workshop classrooms at the middle school level require student independence. Creating and managing this environment can be daunting, but establishing a structure and routines will really help you.

ROOM ARRANGEMENT Keep in mind how you and your students will move about the room. Watch out for tight spaces that could inhibit easy movement. You will also want to set aside space to sit alongside students for conferences. We prefer our students to sit at their desks or tables when they read independently. Finding a special reading nook and getting comfortable is nice, but it isn't necessarily conducive to good thinking and writing. It doesn't matter whether students sit at desks or tables, but they should be able to turn and listen to you and to one another. Also, designate a location where you will meet with small groups of students; groups of three or four students are the most efficient. If possible, get a small table for carrying out small-group work.

Place it in a spot that allows you easy visual and physical access to the room and the rest of your students. Small-group instruction is valuable teaching time, and other students should not come over to interrupt this learning. Establish this rule early in the year. By the time they're in middle school, your students must be able to work independently, solve problems, and stay productive as you meet with small groups or individual students. While the focus of your teaching will be on the small group in front of you, it remains important to keep an eye on other students.

Despite the goal of independence, students will need help with supplies. To save time, have pens, pencils, erasers, and sharpeners in a location that students can easily access.

Many classrooms today have access to technology, but creating your own handwritten charts, posters, and other materials will make your classroom vibrant and personal.

CLASSROOM LIBRARY To entice your kids to read, your classroom library should be accessible, varied, and inviting. Stock it with a variety of texts: fiction and nonfiction books, magazines, and poetry. Reading material should be arranged for easy access, and you should display a wide range of levels, topics, and genres to match the diverse learners in the room. Kids need to read a lot; they will only do that if they are interested in the texts they have access to. Raid your bookshelves at home and visit used-book sales and garage sales.

Keep in mind, as you enhance your library, that the CCSS requires 50 percent of student reading to be in the area of informational text. The good news is that nonfiction texts have been updated—they are cool now. Gone are the encyclopedic texts that were both overwhelming and boring. Today's best nonfiction texts are presented in dynamic ways that entice readers. For example, some informational texts are printed in a picture-book format, but they contain complex ideas, vibrant graphics, and challenging vocabulary. The graphic-novel format is also popular, enabling weaker readers to understand difficult informational and narrative content.

Kids need to be able to find reading material easily, so set out books and other texts in bins or baskets according to author, genre, and/or series. Bins and baskets can be inexpensively purchased at dollar stores or tag sales. Provide a book sign-out sheet like the one shown on page 109 with each bin or basket so students are accountable for returning the material they've checked out.

> ### USING LEVELED BOOKS
>
> Leveled classroom libraries are not essential for independent reading to be successful. In fact, at the middle-school level, obvious labels on texts are a detriment to positive student self-esteem. Another reason that we don't advocate for a leveled library is that the levels are blurred at the middle-school level. Interest in and background knowledge of topics supersede strict reading level.

Planning Instruction

Plan reading instruction over the course of a week. This broad framework will help you organize the goals you want to accomplish. Thinking by the week is less stressful than day-to-day planning/worrying. Thinking ahead to where you want your students to be at the end of the week will make things easier. It's helpful to chunk lessons/skills into manageable pieces throughout the week.

We follow a format that allows for daily independent reading and individual conferences, a mini-lesson on a targeted skill, follow-up independent practice, and small-group instruction as needed. This structure not only supports our planning routine, but it also offers consistency for our students.

We begin each class period with the same routine. After students come into the classroom, they take out their independent reading books, reading logs, and notebooks. We check their logs while students begin reading and taking SmartNotes. After the logs have been checked, we sit alongside students for one-to-one conferences or pull a guided-reading group. After 20 minutes of this independent reading time, we move to whole-class work. Many times, this means that we read aloud from our shared text and take communal SmartNotes. The basic structure is always the same. There is a fluid movement between independent reading and whole-class conversations.

The chart below shows our plan for November 14–18. We were ready to work on a paragraph related to the character traits of Max in *Freak the Mighty*, so our whole-class work was focused there.

	MONDAY	TUESDAY	WEDNESDAY	THURSDAY	FRIDAY
TEACHER	• Log Check • SmartNote Conferences • Mini-Lesson: Using SmartNotes to review thinking around previous chapter of *Freak the Mighty*	• Log Check • Guided Group: Review character traits; make inferences; use Max quotes from *Freak the Mighty*	• Log Check • SmartNote Conferences • Mini-Lesson: Structure for writing about reading: paragraph organizer	• Log Check • Guided Group: Complete paragraph organizers	• Log Check • SmartNote Conferences • Mini-Lesson: Start writing paragraph about Max's character trait from *Freak the Mighty*
STUDENT	• Independent reading with SmartNotes	• Independent reading with SmartNotes • Meet with teacher to work on character traits	• Independent reading with SmartNotes • Work on organizer	• Independent reading with SmartNotes • Meet with teacher to work on organizer	• Independent reading with SmartNotes • Write paragraph

Independent Reading: At the beginning of class, students read their independent reading book and take SmartNotes. The amount of time you can slot for this will depend on your schedule. Our reading classes are 45 minutes long: 20 minutes is devoted to independent reading in grades 5 and 6, while 15 minutes are allocated in grades 7 and 8. On the very first day of class, we establish the habit of students bringing an independent reading book to class each day, so they automatically come in and start reading.

Log Check: As students read, we walk around the classroom and collect information about what students are reading and how much they have read on a Quick Page Inventory Sheet (see page 110). This quick inventory is a pulse check to see if students are really reading at home and maintaining their reading life. Logging page numbers each day both reinforces the importance of maintaining a reading life and helps keep track of how quickly students are moving through books.

Think back to one of Sue's essential questions: *How can I hold students accountable for learning during independent reading?* This question is always in the back of our minds. Maintaining a reading log is a small requirement, yet it is the first step to helping students meet high expectations. They have to read every day, and they have to be able to talk and write about what they have read. This validates independent reading. Their job is to read and think; our job is to check their thinking and support it.

Conferences: Conferences are integral to the independent reading routine. Direct instruction happens at this time. Students can expect a one-on-one conference on a regular basis during independent reading time. These conferences can be a quick check-in of three minutes or a more in-depth conversation of ten minutes. We have the luxury of co-teaching, so we are each able to see three students per day and meet with all our students in a class each week. When we are solo, on the other hand, each of us holds about two conferences per day, so it takes two weeks to meet with all the students. We discuss conferences in Chapter 4.

Mini-Lessons: Mini-lessons are whole-class instruction. They focus on the skills and strategies students need to navigate texts. Mini-lessons come from three different areas.

- Sometimes, after conferring with the whole class, a common need becomes clear. When this happens, we teach a mini-lesson to address this whole-class need.

- Other times, the whole-class-focused mini-lesson comes from what we know our students need at this age/grade level; for example, how to handle complex text structures or character traits.

- Finally, our mini-lesson teaching points come from the work we are doing around a class read-aloud. Students need to transfer these skills to the thinking they do in their independent reading books.

SmartNotes are used in two ways within the mini-lesson. First, we refer to SmartNotes taken as a class when we read a mentor text during shared reading. SmartNotes are also used by students to show us that they are using the strategy we have taught when they read their independent book.

Selecting Just-Right Books for Independent Reading

The essence of independent reading is having each student reading a just-right book—a book that is not too hard and not too easy—and being able to self-select such books. Students learn how to read a book that is a good fit. "Just right" means that the text is of interest to the student and that comprehension requires work but is still accessible independently. This just-right, independent reading book is unquestionably the most important resource for both student and teacher. The chart below is one we create as a class. We discuss the differences between being interested in a book and being able to read it.

A just-right book is that perfect ride: an interesting book that is not too easy nor too hard. So think about interest and readability when you choose a book.	
INTEREST	**READABILITY**
• Read the back cover. • Look at the front cover. • Look at the table of contents. • Read the first page. • Get a recommendation. • Follow a series. • Follow an author. • Follow a genre.	• Read two pages in the middle of the book: Look for words that are too hard. Ask yourself: *Can I think as I read?* • Read the back cover of the book. • Try it!

A problem we often encounter is the desire of middle school students to read long, complex books. These texts are often inappropriate for their age, not to mention above their reading comfort level. Although it is important to challenge students, the just-right book is one that isn't a challenge; it allows readers to both read and think. As a result, reading a just-right book fosters reading growth.

Richard Allington has researched best practices around reading instruction, and a tenet of his work is that readers must read a lot to grow: "First of all, success breeds success. When readers are successful, that success builds all sorts of motivational aspects about reading activity. More reading produces better reading" (2009, p. 50). Growth in reading and time spent reading have a causal relationship; better readers enjoy reading, and therefore, read more. As a result, they grow and become still stronger readers. Weak readers, on the other hand, find reading a struggle and therefore read less—inhibiting their growth. The bottom line is that to grow as a reader, students must read. Students need to be exposed to literature. The right text matters because it supports growth. To refer to these types of texts, Allington has coined the term "high-success reading." This means, "accurate reading, fluent reading, and reading with understanding" (2009, p. 51). Students must be immersed in hearing words, writing words, and reading words.

READING THE SAME BOOK AT SCHOOL AND AT HOME

Consistency is key. Therefore, we ask students to read the same book at home and at school. Following the thread of a longer text is expected of this age group; switching between multiple texts creates confusion. Reading for an extended period of time is practice. It increases students' reading stamina and instills the positive feeling of completing a text and looking forward to the next one. Reading at home and continuing the good work from class is vital to students becoming better readers. To this end, we require students to read for a minimum of 20 minutes a night and to maintain an Independent Reading Log like the one shown on page 111. As mentioned earlier, we check this log daily. A reading log is another record-keeping tool that provides data for the teacher and accountability for the student.

Conclusion

Time spent reading is time well spent. Independent reading is a valuable tool, but it is not an end unto itself. Students shouldn't be "just" sitting and reading—they should be thinking their way through the text—and SmartNotes will help them do that. In the following chapters, you'll read about how to introduce and model SmartNotes to the whole class by working with a core text and how to use it to do on-the-spot assessment and instruction. Reading is active, and SmartNotes prove this.

CHAPTER TWO

SmartNotes: Making Thinking Visible

SmartNotes act as a bridge between the CCSS and independent reading. After delivering instruction, step aside and let your students practice what you've taught by taking SmartNotes as they read independently. Those notes will be proof of their work and the level of thinking they are able to manage independently.

Linking SmartNotes to Reading Instruction Curriculum

The task in front of us is clear: middle school students need to know that they are required to think through texts. They must think, use strategies, and record their thinking. The 15–20 minutes of independent reading time is teaching time. This isn't casual reading; it is work for both you and your students, so you must set clear expectations to make independent reading successful. Students have the job of reading and recording their thinking through SmartNotes, while your job is to monitor this reading and confer. Using a mentor text, we model how to create SmartNotes for the class. After instruction, students are expected to use SmartNotes while reading their independent reading books.

Mentor Texts

Mentor texts are very important in our classroom. Our definition of a mentor text is that it is a sort of textbook; everything we need and want to teach is in that book. When picking a book to read and study, we look for strong characters, beautiful language, accessible conflict, and complex structure. Complex themes make for rich, varied discussions; Newbery Award winners are a great place to start. We make it our business to read the new awardees, to be sure we stay in the know. Another place to look for mentor texts are winners of the National Book Award and the Prinz Award, for older middle school readers.

Gary Paulsen's, *Hatchet*, a Newbery Honor Winner in 1985, is one of our beloved mentor texts. Many fifth graders in the Ardsley Middle School, where we teach, have struggled along with Brian—the book's protagonist—over the years. Brian, a thirteen-year-old boy on his way to visit his father in the Canadian Shield, finds himself stranded after a plane crash. Having to survive alone in this inhospitable setting tests Brian's will, his drive, and his tenacity to live. This modern classic has everything we want in a mentor text: like all people, Brian struggles and changes. The text is accessible, kids understand it, and Gary Paulsen's writing style is truly mesmerizing!

Freak the Mighty by Rodman Philbrick is another one of our favorites. The relationship between the main characters is heart-wrenchingly beautiful. The text is written in first-person so kids can really get to know the characters. Max, the narrator, is a lonely, insecure seventh grader who lives with his grandparents. He is desperate for a friend. When he meets his new next-door neighbor, Freak, his world changes for the better. The two boys overcome much adversity and learn about themselves and what it means to be a friend. Rodman Philbrick's humor, especially when handling delicate situations, grabs students' attention right away.

SUGGESTIONS FOR MENTOR TEXTS

Walk Two Moons by Sharon Creech (realistic fiction)

The View From Saturday by E. L. Konigsburg (realistic fiction)

From the Mixed-Up Files of Mrs. Basil E. Frankweiler by E. L. Konigsburg (realistic fiction)

Catherine, Called Birdy by Karen Cushman (historical fiction)

Shakespeare Bats Clean up by Ron Koertge (novel written in free verse)

Sign of the Beaver by Elizabeth George Speare (historical fiction)

When Zachary Beaver Came to Town by Kimberly Willis Holt (historical fiction)

The Underneath by Kathi Appelt (fantasy)

The Outsiders by S. E. Hinton (realistic fiction)

The Giver by Lois Lowry (science fiction)

Bridge to Terabithia by Katherine Paterson (realistic fiction)

Turtle in Paradise by Jennifer L. Holm (historical fiction)

An American Plague: The True and Terrifying Story of the Yellow Fever Epidemic of 1793 by Jim Murphy (nonfiction)

Bomb: The Race to Build—and Steal—the World's Most Dangerous Weapon by Steve Sheinkin (nonfiction)

Flesh and Blood So Cheap by Albert Marrin (nonfiction)

Amelia Lost: The Life and Disappearance of Amelia Earhart by Candace Fleming (biography)

Night by Elie Wiesel (memoir)

Animal Farm by George Orwell (fiction)

Who Was (series)

Junior Scholastic (magazine)

Cobblestone (magazine)

Dig (magazine)

Faces (magazine)

Throughout the year, we read three mentor texts. These are often read aloud, with students following along in their own copies of the text. At times we ask students to reread the mentor text independently or finish a section on their own. We use the mentor texts to teach our curriculum by modeling reading strategies as we think aloud about a particular passage, exploring vocabulary concepts by analyzing words from the text, discussing literary elements, and noticing the author's style. As we teach, we model our thinking by creating a set of SmartNotes on chart paper and prompt students to add their own thinking.

SMARTNOTE NOTEBOOKS FOR STUDENTS

Students have one notebook that is devoted to recording their SmartNotes. Entries in these notebooks are split between notes on the class mentor text and their independent reading. Students' thinking for the year is archived in these notebooks.

Discussions are also a big part of the reading class. We dictate the pacing as we read the mentor text with students, ensuring that time is spent comprehending the big ideas. Again, we are guiding the topics and modeling our thinking so that students can do this thinking independently. The strategies and skills we impart in this whole-class instruction should carry over into their independent reading; students' SmartNotes will show evidence of this. We have high expectations: after teaching students about the use of literary devices (e.g., personification, metaphor, and simile) we expect them to be able to locate one and discuss its role in their independent book.

Reading Strategies

When *Strategies That Work* (Harvey & Goudvis, 2000) was first published, and then again with its second edition, we both highlighted, bookmarked, and dog-eared its pages. The authors have identified seven distinct reading strategies that readers need to use to be successful when reading fiction or nonfiction, poetry, and texts in the content areas. These strategies are the heart and soul of reading comprehension.

We use a mini-lesson and a mentor text to focus on these strategies, and we expect our students to apply the strategies to their independent reading. Every time students use these strategies, they write them down in the form of a SmartNote in their notebook, which not only shows their thinking but also actually pushes it further. Doing so helps students internalize the strategies and, therefore, become stronger readers. Over time, taking SmartNotes becomes automatic.

Given the focus on nonfiction within the CCSS, it is important to note that the same strategies and skills involved in being a good reader and taker of SmartNotes for fiction apply to nonfiction as well. The CCSS requires readers to comprehend informational texts by determining importance, summarizing, noticing text structure, and author's purpose in a clear, concise way, not by judging. Students use the reading strategies that are all closely tied to the text without doing any wild, personal editorializing. The response should be about the author and the information he or she presents, not about the reader. Students are evaluating the specific text-based evidence and assessing if their reasoning about it is sound. Again, personal opinion is missing. This is a huge departure from fiction, where readers can benefit from personalizing the experience. In reading and thinking about nonfiction, students are asked to take a critical lens to the text—evaluating facts not characters.

We have developed a structured SmartNotes mini-lesson for each strategy as a resource. Each mini-lesson incorporates the use of SmartNotes as a way of cataloging good thinking and showing comprehension. The mini-lesson supports students as they practice applying the strategy. Then, because students record their thinking on the SmartNotes, we can use them as an assessment of this strategy as well.

Since reading nonfiction differs from reading fiction, not all the seven strategies apply to each genre. Reading nonfiction requires close reading. Readers must learn to focus on what the text says and more efficiently use the strategies of summarizing and determining importance. Recording SmartNotes while reading nonfiction is critical because readers must solidify what they know, through writing about it, before moving on and learning new information.

Below are the strategies from Harvey and Goudvis, with our translations.

- **Determining Importance:** When students use this strategy, they notice the difference between important and unimportant details as they navigate texts. Thinking about the importance of information leads to an understanding of the main idea of all texts. Readers are required to sift through information to decide what is important and what isn't. This is a solid, important skill that students need to use to be able to summarize text. Readers rely on this strategy as a way to keep track of information and prove that they know what is going on in a text.

Use with fiction and nonfiction.

- **Making Connections: Text-to-Self**: There are three types of connections that students can make: text-to-self, text-to-text, and text-to-world. The text-to-self connection is the most literal.

  As students read, they notice how and in which ways they relate to the text, including characters, events, and/or conflicts. Writing down "Me Too" SmartNotes fosters students' relationship with the text and characters, allowing them to become more personally invested in reading and eventually gaining a deeper understanding of the text. Initially, just having students note the similarities they have with a character is enough, but relevant connections later extend beyond "Me Too," enabling readers to think about how those connections help them understand their texts and the world.

  Use with fiction. While this strategy supports the reading of fiction, it is less effective in nonfiction. These "Me Too" connections are distracting to readers and take away their focus from the main idea.

- **Visualizing**: Students "see," "feel," "hear," "smell," and "taste" fiction and nonfiction texts to create pictures in their heads. At first, students rely on the sensory adjectives the author uses to do this, but ultimately, strong visualizers use these pictures to make inferences about characters. Visualizing SmartNotes are a favorite with students; everyone can easily take this kind of note.

  Use with fiction and nonfiction.

- **Asking Relevant Questions**: As readers notice what they are wondering about as they read, they are encouraged to think about what truly matters in the text. Although many students will ask literal questions, which ultimately will be answered in the next pages, we prompt them to ask questions that require work—inferential thinking—to answer. Students can return to their original SmartNotes once they find answers. Asking questions is one way for readers to stay engaged in their reading. "Why" questions often help students think more deeply. Keeping track of their questions supports readers in two ways:

  1. Writing down questions allows students to pinpoint places in the text that are confusing or that make them wonder.

  2. When rereading questions, students are able to categorize and organize them to formulate thoughts on theme or the author's message.

  There are two main types of questions: closed and open. *Closed questions* have answers that can easily be answered as readers continue through the text. *Open questions* require readers to make inferences to find the answers. Both types of questions are important for readers; however, closed questions lend themselves to literal thinking, whereas open questions lead to inferential thinking.

  Use with fiction and nonfiction.

- **Predicting**: This strategy requires students to ask, "What happens next?" A good prediction is one in which students take what has already happened in the text and imagine what will happen as a result. Wild predictions, although entertaining—and, unfortunately, frequent—do not help readers. Taking Prediction SmartNotes is fun for students. Imagining the future of the text encourages readers to be thoughtful.
  Use primarily with fiction.

- **Making Connections: Text-to-text**: Readers notice how the text they are reading relates to other texts or media they have read or seen.
  Use with fiction and nonfiction.

- **Making Connections: Text-to-world**: Readers connect the text they are reading to events they know about in the world.
  Use with fiction and nonfiction.

- **Inferring**: This is the King of Strategies! Readers who can infer can go far. Strong readers don't just rely on the words in the text; they think beyond it. Inferring means "reading between the lines." When readers infer, they take information from the text and add it to their own background knowledge, which helps them figure out information the author hasn't provided. All higher level, analytical thinking requires this kind of thought. This strategy is hard, but it comes with practice and guidance. Inference SmartNotes prove smart thinking.
  Use with fiction and nonfiction.

- **Synthesizing**: Students create new information based on a text they have read. They accumulate knowledge as they read and then synthesize it to come up with an original idea. Think of this as a giant inference where the information from a text is evaluated after a large chunk of it has been read—often at the end. Looking back on all the Inference SmartNotes taken, students reflect and are able to say something "big" about their thinking and the text. The result of this thinking is a Synthesis SmartNote.
  Use with fiction and nonfiction.

We've added the following strategies because they help us meld strategy-based reading instruction with the study of a text:

- **Summarizing:** This strategy is foundational. If readers cannot say in their own words what they have read, they are not fully understanding the text. A good Summary SmartNote is a precursor to higher order reading strategies.
  Use with fiction and nonfiction.

- **Clarifying Confusion**: This strategy is a good combination of determining importance and asking questions. When readers notice that they had been thinking incorrectly, they can reference their SmartNotes to pinpoint where they got off track. This strategy often requires students to reread, and their SmartNotes show them where to begin rereading.
  Use with fiction and nonfiction.

- **Using Text Features:** It is important for readers to notice how a writer uses text features, especially in nonfiction. SmartNoting text features, including boldface words, text boxes, captions, charts, and maps, encourage readers to pay attention and notice how the features support their understanding of the big idea.

- **Literary Devices**: Exposing students to literary devices, such as simile, metaphor, personification, flashback, foreshadowing, theme, and symbolism, helps them notice when an author employs these devices. Additionally, readers understand why the author used the device—how it helps them better understand the text. SmartNotes are perfect for this strategy. Every time students detect a device being used, they record it, which allows them to reflect on the purpose of the device.

- **Six Traits of Writing: Ideas, Organization, Voice, Sentence Fluency, Word Choice, Conventions**: Through our work with the carefully chosen mentor texts—where the focus on craft is natural—students then begin to notice the unique writing style in their own independent texts. After noticing, for example, Gary Paulsen's use of one-word sentences/paragraphs in the whole-class lesson on *Hatchet*, readers look for short sentences in the books they are reading independently. Taking 6-Trait SmartNotes encourages a rich examination of a text.

Conclusion

We used to want to believe that all students entering middle school were already very familiar with these reading strategies. We were also naive enough to assume that they would be able to name and define these strategies. Then reality sank in: Students need direct instruction in these reading strategies.

It is worthwhile and important for students to know the kinds of thinking they are doing. SmartNoting the text as they read makes their thinking visible. This allows you to compliment students and label their thinking, which not only deepens comprehension, but it also strengthens their confidence. Students think: *I can read this; I know how to think.* Taking SmartNotes makes them feel smart.

Reading Is Thinking: Launching SmartNotes

During the first week of school, we emphasize that independent reading is a valued, critical component of our class. We provide students with an outline of the class routine, their own independent reading texts, and a mission to read and love books. The stage is set for instruction.

In the second week of school, we introduce SmartNotes and the teaching of strategies. For the next six weeks, we teach SmartNote strategies through modeling with a mentor text and having students practice as they read independently. As the year progresses, we spiral back through each strategy, depending on student needs, through whole-class mini-lessons as well as individual conferences and small groups.

To introduce SmartNotes, we use a reading-about-thinking-conversation. We ask our students the following question: "What does 'reading is thinking' mean to you?" Then Sue demonstrates a distracted reader, focusing on anything other than her book. We have been at this for a while, so we know what middle schoolers are thinking about during independent reading: lunch, soccer practice, math test, fight with Mom, lunch, who to sit with at lunch, science lab, lunch.

Kids love this demonstration. After their giggles subside, we ask them to generate a list of what good readers think about when they read. We are honest with them. We tell students we know that thinking is hard work and that every reader will sometimes lose focus and that our goal is to get them to the place where they think of reading as thinking.

Then we work with students to create a "What Do Readers Think About When They Read?" chart. To get kids going, Betsy gently reminds them, "Lunch doesn't count." Students talk about and describe what readers do as they read, and we record the strategy and its description on the chart. They might say, for example, "I make a picture in my head." Our reply would be, "Yes, readers make pictures in their heads. This is called visualizing." We list all the strategies that students suggest and add others we want to bring to their attention. Finally, we introduce SmartNotes by telling students that they are a written record of their thinking when they read. We add that information to the chart and explain that each reading-thinking strategy listed on the chart is a type of SmartNote they can take as they read. Because of this, from this day forward, we refer to the chart as the "SmartNote Chart." A sample chart appears on the next page.

The creation of this chart is phase one. After creating the chart and discussing the strategies, phase two, our Readers Workshop, begins. Our 45-minute workshop block looks like this:

- **15 Minutes of Independent Reading:** During this time students take SmartNotes and practice the strategy. Strategy instruction has been delivered through one-on-one conferences and small, guided groups. During the "Practice through independent reading" portion of the mini-lesson, we meet with students. The goal is to meet with each student at least once a week through either one-on-one conferences or small-guided groups. More information on conferences and guided groups appears in Chapters 4 and 5.

- **15 Minutes of Strategy Instruction:** We model our whole-class instruction using a mentor text. The mentor text is our class text; we teach everything through these texts.

- **10 Minutes of Independent Practice:** Students read independently and practice using the new strategy by writing SmartNotes.

- **5 Minutes of Sharing SmartNotes and Closing the Lesson:** We ask several students to share their SmartNotes and then close the lesson. Often we close a lesson by having a student volunteer to share a specific SmartNote that exemplifies the mini-lesson; for example, "We just practiced taking Visualizing SmartNotes. Who would like to share one they took with the class?"

Until students become proficient SmartNote takers, we prompt them at the start of independent reading to "notice when you are thinking and write down your thoughts."

Reading Strategy Mini-Lessons

Mini-lessons are an important part of the reading block. They are the short, focused, and targeted instruction that will benefit your entire class of readers. Each mini-lesson centers around a mentor text—a text we love. A mentor text might be a newspaper or magazine article or a fiction or informational book. These texts inspire conversation and thought. As we read aloud the mentor text, we and our students notice many things: characters, plot, setting, great words, interesting structure, details, maps and other graphics, headings, and illustrations. All these observations make their way into our class SmartNotes because we know that when students read their own books, they will need to think about all those elements to fully understand the text. As we savor this mentor text, we are using it as a tool to teach our curriculum.

Our mini-lessons are composed of the following five components:

1. **Explain the purpose of instruction:** We start by explaining the purpose of the instruction, the ways in which it will help students as readers.

2. **Demonstrate the strategy in action:** Then we model the skill. We demonstrate how we, as readers, use it. We mostly rely on our mentor text for modeling. This text and students' notebooks are the only materials required.

WHAT DO READERS THINK ABOUT WHEN THEY READ?

What does "reading is thinking" mean?

What SHOULD you be thinking about as you read???

- CHARACTERS
  What they are doing and *why*?

- PROBLEM/CONFLICT
  What is it?
  Solution

- PREDICTIONS

- REMEMBER/RECOGNIZE/UNDERSTAND IMPORTANT EVENTS

- SETTING
  Why is setting important?

- PLOT: WHAT IS HAPPENING?

- REREAD

- MAKE INFERENCES: READ BETWEEN THE LINES

- MAKE CONNECTIONS
  Text-to-Text
  Text-to-Self
  Text-to-World

- VISUALIZE: MAKE PICTURES IN YOUR MIND

- ASK QUESTIONS

- NOTICE AUTHOR'S STYLE

- UNDERSTAND MESSAGE: THEME

- SUMMARIZE

             STOP and THINK

Every time you think, you must write it down:
Quote from Book (page number)
+ Your Thinking (Strategy) = SmartNotes

3. Interact with the text: After modeling, we give students a chance to dig into the text to practice the strategy with us.

4. Practice through independent reading: Then students practice independently through their independent reading texts.

5. Share: Finally, we end the lesson by asking students to share their good thinking.

Placing Strategies on a Continuum

We like to think of the reading strategies as being on a continuum ranging from the most literal thinking to the most inferential thinking. The CCSS curriculum requires students to be nimble thinkers who can flow smoothly between strategies. Our mini-lesson sequence follows this continuum, each building on the previously taught skill as the chart at the right shows.

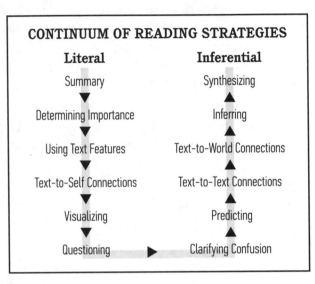

CONTINUUM OF READING STRATEGIES

Literal	Inferential
Summary	Synthesizing
Determining Importance	Inferring
Using Text Features	Text-to-World Connections
Text-to-Self Connections	Text-to-Text Connections
Visualizing	Predicting
Questioning	Clarifying Confusion

Sample Mini-Lessons

The order in which we teach the mini-lessons follows the reading strategy continuum above. A sample mini-lesson for each strategy, correlated to the CCSS, appears below. We've chosen texts for each sample that are appropriate and accessible for middle school students in grades 5–8. Keep in mind that you will need to gauge your students' understanding of the strategies. In some cases, students will need only one mini-lesson to understand a strategy, but in other cases, multiple lessons around a single strategy may be necessary.

MINI-LESSON

SUMMARY

We start with Summary SmartNotes instruction. This is a great way to begin the year. Summary is a solid building-block strategy that is effective with fiction and nonfiction. Students are asked to sift through what they have learned from their text and condense it into a few sentences. They are taught how important it is to understand and know what they read. Summary SmartNoting sets up the harder, more inferential strategies that come later. Because it is a literal-thinking strategy, starting with Summary makes sense.

Summary SmartNotes Mini-Lesson for Fiction

CCSS RL.5.2, RL.6.2, RL.7.2, RL.8.2

MATERIALS

- Mentor text: *Freak the Mighty* by Rodman Philbrick (teacher copy and one copy for each student)
- Chart paper and markers or whiteboard (dry-erase or interactive) with markers
- Student notebooks and pencils

STEP 1 Explain the purpose of instruction.

Summarizing is a strategy that helps readers focus on the big ideas instead of extraneous information. Students learn how to think through a text and write down what is important using SmartNotes.

Sue: Taking SmartNotes helps you keep track of what is going on in your book. Today, we are starting *Freak the Mighty*, and it is a long book. Remembering what is happening in the text and what is important will help us all think smartly through the book. Take a look at the SmartNotes Chart. We are going to practice taking Summary SmartNotes. Summarizing is a good way for us to keep track of the important events and characters we learn about in our reading.

STEP 2 Demonstrate the strategy in action.

(Sue reads the first few pages of *Freak the Mighty* aloud, stopping at the end of page 3.)

Sue: I am going to stop now, because that was a lot of information and I need to think about what I know so far. Okay, who is telling the story? It was confusing at first; I just figured out after the last paragraph that Max is the one telling the story. Let's write this down: *The "I" is Max.* Who is the other person?

Haley: Freak?

Sue: That's right. I wonder . . . could that be his real name? Even though I have read only three pages, we have learned a lot about Max. Let's write down what the author has told us about Max in a Summary SmartNote. When you are taking a Summary SmartNote, you always begin by listing the main characters and what you learn about them in the first few pages. In your notebook, you would write a quote from the book that tells you about the character, and the page number. Watch me and then copy it into your notebook.

(Sue writes quotes from the text on the board, and students copy them in their own notebooks.)

"Called me Kicker."(p. 1)

"I had a thing about booting anyone who dared to touch me." (p. 2)

From these quotes, we know that Kicker is Max and that he doesn't like to be hugged or touched— interesting. I'm going to write down my thinking about the quote.

(Sue writes her thoughts on the board, and students copy them into their notebooks.)

Kicker is Max, and he doesn't like to be hugged or touched.

STEP 3 Interact with the text.

(Sue continues reading and stopping to engage students in thinking about the text.)

Sue: Let's make a list of the characters we have met so far.

Alex: Gram and Grim.

Sue: Who are they? Let's write this down in our SmartNotes:

Gram and Grim are the grandmother and grandfather.

Olivia: Freak.

Sue: Who is he?

Olivia: I don't know, I think another kid in pre-school.

(Sue writes: *Freak—? Kid in school?*)

Sue: What else do we know about Freak?

Jason (shrugs): He has crutches?

Sue: Let's add that: *Freak has crutches—why?*

Let's reread the end of page two to learn more about him.

(Sue rereads through page 2, with a focus on learning more about the character Freak.)

Sue: What else did we learn?

Sam: He has braces strapped to his crooked legs.

Sue: Let's add that to our SmartNotes: *Freak has crooked legs with braces. (p. 2)*

STEP **4** Practice through independent reading.

(Sue gives students the assignment for the day.)

Sue: Okay everyone—that was great thinking. When you go back to your independent books in a moment, we want you to try this work. As you read, write down what you have learned. These Summary SmartNotes will help you keep track of your thinking and keep you from getting confused.

(As students read independently, Sue and Betsy check in with as many readers as they can.)

STEP **5** Share.

(Sue calls an end to independent reading in preparation for sharing.)

Sue: Okay, guys, find a good place to stop. Who wants to share some of their good thinking?

Maggie: I'm reading *The Mixed-Up Files of Mrs. Basil E. Frankweiler*, and my Summary SmartNote is that Claudia and Jaime are trying to figure out the mystery of Angel. It is really important to Claudia that the statue is really Michelangelo's.

(During a conference, if we notice that one or two students have done a particularly good job with the strategy, we ask him or her to share at this point to close the lesson.)

Sue: Great job. Jordan, let's hear from you.

(Jordan responds, and we ask another student to share as well.)

SUMMARY SMARTNOTES SAMPLE

To give you a sense of a variety of Summary SmartNotes, we have included a few samples from fifth- and sixth-grade readers on the next page. All this thinking, supported by text evidence, indicates readers who are making sense of their reading.

Independent Reading in the Age of Common Core © 2013 by Sue Cannone-Calick & Elizabeth Henley • Scholastic Teaching Resources

> 9/14 __Project Mulberry__
>
> P.112. Julia and Patrick ask Kenny to write down the temperatures for the sake of the silkworms. The eggs get bigger in 15 days, and Patrick sets up a camera. The black dots (periods) in the eggs became commas.
>
> P.115 Julia and Patrick went to Mr. Dixon's to get more leaves for the silkworms. They weeded his garden to thank him. He came out with lemonade and brownies and they all shared storys.

> 25 " Edmund and the wardrobe" (title)
> • will he go to Narnia?
> • will he meat Mr. Tumnus?
> • will he meat another Animal person

> 12/31/10 __Schooled__
> Cap is a smart boy, but he learned stuff from a different point of view. He wasn't great in his academics. He didn't know what TV, ipads, public school looked like.
>   In Claverage Middle School, (C Average Middle school), they pick the most clueless kid and play pranks on him/her. Cap was elected and he won. Zach, Lena, and Naomi the popular kids played pranks like giving him fake directions. Naomi made up a 7th grader who wrote 'love' letters to Cap.
>   Cap really hates it and wants to go home.
>   Will he become a 'normal'

GRADE 5:

(top left) Lauren, a solid reader, is reading Project Mulberry by Linda Sue Park. Notice that she stops and writes a summary note every few pages, and as a result, she makes sense of this text and we can clearly see that.

(top right) Sam uses his summary to ask thoughtful questions as he navigates The Lion, the Witch and the Wardrobe by C. S. Lewis.

GRADE 6:

(bottom right) Samantha uses her summary to make inferences and ask questions as she reads Schooled by Gordon Korman.

MINI-LESSON

DETERMINING IMPORTANCE

Our next SmartNotes mini-lesson on Determining Importance is closely connected to the Summary mini-lesson. After spending a few days on summary, it becomes clear that not all students are focusing on the important information (e.g., facts, charts, graphs, and details). Determining Importance SmartNotes require readers to separate relevant from irrelevant information. Students practice Determining Importance for a few weeks; switching back to Summary SmartNotes once in a while. These linked strategies are ideal to follow one another and bounce between. Being a good summarizer solidifies a reader's ability to determine importance, and being a strong determiner of importance leads to the production of a complete summary.

Determining Importance SmartNotes Mini-Lesson for Fiction

(CCSS) RL.5.1, RL.5.2, RL.6.1, RL.6.2, RL.7.1, RL.7.2, RL.8.1, RL.8.2

> **MATERIALS**
> • Mentor text: *Animal Farm* by George Orwell (teacher copy and one copy for each student)
> • Chart paper and markers or whiteboard (dry-erase or interactive) with markers
> • Student notebooks and pencils

STEP 1 · Explain the purpose of instruction.

When we ask students to determine importance, we are asking them to sift through all the information the author provides and figure out what is most important—the main idea. Having to keep lots of extraneous information in one's head contributes to confusion. Proficient readers know what information to let go of. This sifting enables deeper understanding of the text.

(This eighth-grade class spent many weeks learning about the Russian Revolution and reading allegories in preparation for reading *Animal Farm*. As we started reading this mentor text, we made many SmartNotes about the information in it and allegorical connections. We took about 12 SmartNotes in all.)

Betsy: Before we even started this book, we spent weeks learning about the Russian Revolution and communism and socialism. We talked about how different socialism is from democracy. This is a lot of information to remember. We've also just read the first two chapters of *Animal Farm*, and that, too, contained a lot of information. As readers, we need to prioritize what we focus on in a text—if we try to hold onto too much information, we'll become confused.

STEP 2 · Demonstrate the strategy in action.

Betsy: Let's sift through all the SmartNotes on this novel that we've taken so far.

(Students grumble—that's a lot of sifting!)

Betsy: I know, but we have to remember what we know so far so we can focus on what is important. There are lots of small details in our SmartNotes: No one can find Moses the crow; Old Major dies; the animals overthrow Mr. Jones and the men; Molly is worried that she won't get ribbons now that the animals have taken over; Napoleon and Snowball become the leaders of the farm; they learn to read and write and create the seven commandments. Some of these details are more important than others. I think, for example, that it doesn't matter that Molly is worried about ribbons. What's more important is that Snowball and Napoleon have taken over and that they've learned to be like men and read and write. I can tell those details are more important because they lead me to the big idea that most people, and animals in this case, are looking to be led.

David: That's hard!

Betsy: Yes, it is, but let's think it through together.

STEP 3 · Interact with the text.

(Betsy reads aloud the first two pages of chapter 3.)

Betsy: We just read a lot of details—which ones are important?

Samantha: The hens and ducks gathered all the stalks, and no animals steal food.

Betsy: You pulled out two important details, but rather than remembering these specific things, remember instead why these details are important. Why does it matter that the ducks did that?

Daniel: I agree with Sammie. The details matter because each animal did what he could. The ducks used their beaks to pick up stalks—it was smart.

Betsy: Exactly, that's the big idea. If we all remember that at the beginning of the summer everything went well on the farm because each animal did his part and no one stole, we don't need to hold onto all the little details that go into that. This is powerful and smart thinking. This is important; we need to SmartNote it.

(Betsy records the SmartNote below, and students record it in their notebooks.)

"There was no wastage whatever; the hens and ducks with their sharp eyes had gathered up the very last stalk." (p. 46) *Each animal does his part. This helps the farm run smoothly. Everything is going well at the start of the summer when the animals have taken over. The big idea here is that when everyone pulls his weight, things run smoothly.*

Remember, the hens and ducks themselves are not important, so you can let those details go.

STEP 4 Practice through independent reading.

Betsy: We will pick up where we left off in chapter 3 of *Animal Farm* tomorrow. Now it's time for independent reading. When you are reading, focus your SmartNotes on the details that support the main idea. Keep track of details that help you figure out the big ideas, and let the other details go.

(Sue and Betsy conduct one-on-one conferences while students read.)

STEP 5 Share.

(Betsy transitions from independent reading to sharing.)

Betsy: Good work everyone; does anyone want to share a SmartNote?

Carly: I want to share! I'm reading *Prom and Prejudice*, and I love it. It doesn't matter that Lizzy has to work in a coffee shop, but it does matter that unlike everyone else at her posh boarding school, she has to have a job.

Betsy: I love that book, too! Good thinking. Thanks for sharing.

DETERMINING IMPORTANT INFORMATION SMARTNOTES SAMPLES

GRADE 5:

Harris is reading Shredderman: Attack of the Tagger *by Wendelin Van Draanen, and he organizes a suspect list to help keep track of what is important in the text.*

Sam is reading Harry Potter and the Goblet of Fire *by J. K. Rowling. He makes a chart to categorize the main characters and compare them to himself.*

Determining Importance SmartNotes Mini-Lesson for Nonfiction

Determining Importance is also a valuable strategy when reading nonfiction. In the reading of nonfiction, using the strategy of Summary along with Determining Importance is a useful combination to make sense of the text.

CCSS RI.5.1, RI.5.2, RI.6.1, RI.6.2, RI.7.1, RI.7.2, RI.8.1, RI.8.2

> **MATERIALS**
> - Mentor texts: "A Car for the Masses" and "Let There Be Light" from *Cobblestone* (teacher copy and one copy for each student)
> - Chart paper and markers or whiteboard (dry-erase or interactive) with markers
> - Student notebooks and pencils

STEP 1 Explain the purpose of instruction.

This lesson will tackle the challenge of sifting through information to focus on the central/main idea. Separating relevant from irrelevant information is difficult. Students need to learn to discriminate between what is interesting or cool versus what is central to the big idea.

STEP 2 Demonstrate the strategy in action.

(Sue displays a copy of "A Car for the Masses" on the interactive whiteboard and hands the articles to students.)

Sue: Today we are going to read an article about the Model T Ford. Thinking about where our cars came from is cool. They have come a long way! The author is going to give us a lot of information. It will be our job as readers to figure out what is important in the article and what are just interesting facts. As I read aloud to you, we will need to figure out what the big idea of this text is and learn to let go of nonessential information.

(Sue reads aloud the opening quote from Henry Ford, and then the first two paragraphs of the article.)

In this section of the article, we learned about Ford's vision, and what travel was like in the early 1900s. I think the important part of this section is that Ford wanted to make a car. (Sue underlines quotes from those two paragraphs: "car for the great multitude," "travel was difficult," "relied on horses," "roads were dirt paths.") I am underlining these three quotes on the interactive whiteboard, and you should underline the same quotes on your copy. Together, these quotes support the big idea that Ford wanted to make a great car for all Americans. (In the margin, Sue records the main idea, and asks students to copy the information on their copies.) Let's read on and notice if this big idea continues to be supported in the text.

STEP 3 Interact with the text.

(Sue reads the next two paragraphs and stops.)

Sue: I have to stop. Listen to this again: "After years of tinkering and testing—and working his way through the alphabet—Ford introduced his Model T in 1908." That is so cool! I didn't know that was how Ford named his cars. I knew there was a Model A—but I didn't know there were models named after all those other letters. This is an interesting fact, but is it important to the main idea? (Sue asks students to reread and gives them two minutes to think about this quietly.)

Sue: Is this fact part of the main idea?

(When no one replies, Sue takes another tack.)

Sue: Let's figure this out. Let's go back to what we underlined and wrote at the beginning of the article. Is knowing that the cars are named in alphabetical order important to the fact that Ford wanted to make a car for all Americans?

Kids: NO!

Sue: Since this does not support the main idea, it is not essential information; therefore, it is irrelevant, and we shouldn't underline it.

(Sue continues to read to the end the next paragraph.)

Sue: What facts did we learn that support the main idea?

Bobby: Before Ford, cars were expensive. Then he used an assembly line to make cars cheaper.

Sue: Come up to the whiteboard and highlight that fact for us. As Bobby highlights this on the board, be sure you are underlining it on your copy.

(Bobby comes up to the board and highlights the information on page 13.)

Sue: Let's talk about how that fact supports the central idea that Ford wanted a car for all Americans.

Bobby: Making cars cheaper means more people can buy them.

Sue: Excellent. Everyone, let's record this in the margins. Can anyone else find facts to further support the main idea that Ford wanted to make cars for all Americans to buy?

Cynthia: It says, "More Americans could afford to buy his low-priced automobiles."

Sue: Well done. Cynthia, come highlight that fact on the whiteboard. Everyone else—be sure to underline on your copy.

(Sue finishes reading the text.)

Sue: Please underline facts that support the central idea. (Sue gives students about three minutes to do this.) Now that you have done that, in your notebooks, create a SmartNote using a quote from the text to support the big idea and include your own thinking.

(Sue gives students ten minutes to work and then asks for a volunteer to share.)

Vinny: Here is my SmartNote: "The Model T changed the way Americans lived." My thinking is: *Henry Ford was a smart man. He made a car that helped people do lots of things like work and travel.*

Sue: Yes, and did all of you notice how Vinny made this SmartNote about the text, and not his impressions? Good close reading, Vinny.

STEP 4 Practice through independent reading.

(Sue distributes a copy of "Let There Be Light" to each student.)

Sue: For the next 20 minutes, you will work independently to do a close reading of the article, "Let There Be Light." Remember to focus on what is relevant and irrelevant in the article like we did with "A Car for the Masses."

(Students start to read and underline independently. Sue sits alongside a table of students and checks in on the underlining they are doing every few paragraphs. She does this as a group instead of individual conferences so she can touch base with more students at one time.)

STEP 5 Share.

(After about 20 minutes, Sue observes that all the students have completed their reading and underlining.)

Sue: Who would like to share the main idea they found in the article?

Cassie: I thought the main idea was that the light bulb made things better for people.

Sue: What do you guys think? Does that make sense?

Students: Yes!

Sue: Okay, at your table, share a fact that supports this idea. (Sue asks for a volunteer to share a fact.)

Adam (reads): ". . . they tried a light bulb with carbonized cotton sewing thread. It glowed for more than thirteen hours." (p. 13)

Sue: How does that support the main idea?

Adam: Thirteen hours is a long time, considering that light used to come from candles that didn't last that long.

Sue: Good point. Let's make this a SmartNote. I will write it on the board, and each of you needs to record it in your notebook.

(Sue and each student record Adam's quote and the page number. Then she adds their thinking: *Having light for a long time was an important improvement in the lives of Americans.*)

Using Text Features SmartNotes Mini-Lesson for Nonfiction

RI.5.5, RI.6.5, RI.7.5, RI.8.5

MATERIALS
- Mentor texts: "A Car for the Masses," "Let There Be Light," and *The Trouble Begins at 8* by Sid Fleischman (teacher copy and one copy for each student)
- Chart paper and markers or whiteboard (dry-erase or interactive) with markers
- Student notebooks and pencils

STEP 1 Explain the purpose of instruction.

Readers must take into account all the information that is presented to them. When reading informational text, they must use the structures of the text to help ensure their comprehension. This lesson encourages readers to look at all parts of an informational text (all those features that students often overlook) to glean important information that enhances the big idea.

(Students have already read two of these articles in the previous mini-lesson on determining importance. We now want them to pay attention to how the text is put together—text features and structures—so they can enhance their understanding of the main idea.)

Betsy: As I pull up yesterday's articles, "A Car for the Masses," and "Let There Be Light," please find your copies.

Maggie: I thought we were done with them!

Betsy: There is so much more to notice and think about! Today we are going to notice how this text is organized and put together.

STEP 2 Demonstrate the strategy in action.

(Betsy waits until everyone has the article in front of them.)

Betsy: Yesterday, when we read this article, we focused on figuring out the big idea. We pulled facts from all over the text to support our thinking. We determined that the big idea was that Ford wanted to create a car for all Americans. Today, we are going to make sure we have noticed all parts of the text and see if those parts confirm our understanding. Let's focus on the quote at the top of the page: Henry Ford's own words. Did anyone notice that the quote is in a different font?

Class: OHHH!

(Betsy reads the Henry Ford quote from the article.)

Betsy: I know that many of you often skip over text like that when you are reading nonfiction!

(Giggles from the class.)

Betsy: All the information presented in nonfiction text is important to read. Quotes, captions, fact/vocabulary boxes, maps, diagrams, and illustrations all contain information readers need. Often, in fact, the information in these text features is essential to support your understanding of the main idea. Again, the main idea in this article is that Ford wanted to create a car for everyone. Readers can find the main idea in Ford's own words. His vision is the main idea of the article. The author then used additional facts to support the main idea. What other features help support the main idea?

Derek: There is a picture of a Model T car and a caption.

(Betsy circles the picture and caption on the whiteboard and asks students to do the same on their copy.)

Betsy: What do we learn from those two features?

Derek: The caption says that Henry Ford created the assembly line to make cars cheaper so everyone could have one.

Betsy: Great!

STEP 3 Interact with the text.

(Betsy pulls the article "Let There be Light" up on the whiteboard and prepares students to think about text features.)

Betsy: Now look at your copy of "Let There Be Light." Which text features do you notice in this article?

Diana: There is a vocabulary box, a photograph, and a diagram.

Betsy: Yes, and each picture comes with a caption as well. Why is it important for you to not skip these features?

Diana: I know. I bet they will have important information I will need.

Betsy: The big idea for this article is that the light bulb changed Americans' lives. Do these text features support this idea?

All: YES!

Betsy: Can someone come up and highlight aspects of the text features that support the main idea?

(Larry raises his hand and then comes to the board. He highlights a word in the photo caption.)

Larry: I think the word "tinkering" from the photo caption is important because it shows that Edison worked on the light bulb for a long time.

Betsy: True. How does this support the big idea?

Larry: It shows that he believed that if he made the light bulb good, it would be worth it for people.

Betsy: Let's SmartNote this good thinking: *"tinkering" shows how Edison worked on the light bulb for a long time.*

STEP 4 Practice through independent reading.

Betsy: Today's independent reading is the text, *The Trouble Begins at 8.* As you read, remember to notice text features and how they support your determination of this article's main idea.

(Betsy distributes copies of the text and allows students 15 minutes to read and notice features. While students work, Betsy and Sue make sure readers are on task and answer questions.)

STEP 5 Share.

(Betsy calls the class back together and asks students to share their thinking.)

Simon: The big idea of the text was that Twain went on a lecture tour for money. He used humor to connect with the audience.

Betsy: NICE! What text features support your thinking?

Simon: There are three of his quotes stuck on the corners of the pages that are funny.

Betsy: Good job! The humor was tucked away in the corner, but you noticed it!

MINI-LESSON

TEXT-TO-SELF CONNECTIONS

Next, we teach students to make powerful text-to-self connections. As stated previously, we only practice this strategy with fiction, as it is not a strong informational text strategy. The entire set of connection strategies—text-to-self, text-to-text, text-to-world—is taught in three separate mini-lessons throughout our six-week SmartNote launch. Although text-to-self is relatively accessible to students, text-to-text thinking assumes readers have a wider range of reading experiences than many students will have at this juncture, and text-to-world requires more inferential thinking.

Our focus on text-to-self connections is the first mini-lesson that brings readers into SmartNotes in a very personal way. Students gravitate easily to this kind of thinking. In fact, the independent reading books they choose tend to reflect personal connections, and they are eager to explore the text. The teaching here is to ensure that the connections push greater understanding of the text and are not merely "me too" thinking.

Text-to-Self Connections
SmartNotes Mini-Lesson for Fiction

(CCSS) **RL.5.1, RL.5.3, RL.6.1, RL.6.3, RL.7.1, RL.7.3, RL.8.1, RL.8.3**

> **MATERIALS**
> • Mentor text: *Hatchet* by Gary Paulsen (teacher copy and one copy for each student)
> • Chart paper and markers or whiteboard (dry-erase or interactive) with markers
> • Student notebooks and pencils

STEP 1 Explain the purpose of the instruction.

Recognizing themselves in the characters they encounter helps students think differently and more deeply about the character's personality, choices, conflicts, and eventually, how they solve their problems.

(We have been reading *Hatchet* for two weeks.)

Betsy: None of us has ever been stranded in the Canadian Shield, but we know that we have felt some of the same emotions as Brian. Like Brian, we have all felt abandoned in some way; we have all been haunted by a memory that we can't get rid of. Connecting to Brian is one way of understanding him and what he is going through. Writing Text-to-Self Connection SmartNotes gives us time and a place to reflect. Thinking about Brian helps us understand him and a little bit more about ourselves.

STEP 2 Demonstrate the strategy in action.

Betsy: Let's start by rereading the class SmartNotes we took yesterday. Page 76 of the book was very powerful. Brian was stabbed with porcupine needles. From what we discussed yesterday, we know that Brian is in a bad way. Here's our SmartNote quote: "The pain filled his leg now and with it came new waves of self-pity. Sitting alone in the dark, his leg aching, some mosquitoes finding him again, he started crying" (p. 76).

Now let's add our thinking to our SmartNote. Brian is feeling awful. He is sad, in pain, and crying about it. This is the first time he is crying—wow! Raise your hand if you have ever felt like this. I will write it on the board, and you should add thinking to your SmartNote in your notebook: *Brian is very sad.* Let's keep reading.

(Betsy reads aloud to the end of page 77.)

Betsy: All of us, Brian included, just learned something important. Let's write down our thinking. (On the whiteboard, Betsy adds her thinking to the SmartNote quote: *Brian cried and cried and cried and finally realized that self-pity would get him nowhere.* Students copy it in their notebooks.)

STEP 3 Interact with the text.

Betsy: Can you make a connection here? I can. I know that sometimes, when I am done crying and stomping my feet—I still feel sad, but nothing has changed, I still have to clean my house, I still need to grade papers, I still need to cook dinner. Think about a time when you were sad, and even after crying or having a temper tantrum, your problem was still not solved. You realized you had to do something to solve the problem. Let's start a Connection SmartNote.

(Betsy writes the following quote on the whiteboard: "When he sat alone in the darkness and cried and was done, all done with it, nothing had changed. His leg still hurt, it was still dark, he was still alone and the self-pity had accomplished nothing." (p. 77). Students copy it in their notebook.)

Betsy: Below this quote, write about a time you felt the same way.

(Betsy and Sue walk around and read over students' shoulders to see the connections they are making and recording.)

STEP 4 Practice through independent reading.

Betsy: Good work. By watching Brian cope with his difficulties, we, as readers, can learn how to cope with our own. That is the power of connections. Okay, everyone, when you are reading your independent reading books, please pay attention to any connections you are able to make. Think about our work with Brian. You don't have to share everything with the character—it could be a feeling, a thought, or a situation. We will have conferences, and at the end of the period, we will share.

STEP 5 Share.

(After about 20 minutes of independent reading and SmartNoting along with conferences, Betsy pulls the class back together.)

Betsy: Who would like to share their Connection SmartNote?

Elliot: I am reading *Eragon* by Christopher Paolini, and even though I have obviously never had a pet dragon, I have had a dog, and I know that it is hard to care for a pet.

Betsy: Exactly—even though your life is not the same as in *Eragon*, your connection helps you understand him better.

TEXT-TO-SELF CONNECTIONS SMARTNOTES SAMPLES

GRADE 6:

(left) Geoffrey, a strong reader, makes sense of the nonfiction book Baseball Codes *by Jason Turbow, by using his personal knowledge of baseball as he reads.*

(right) Heenal uses her text-to-self connection to visualize a scene in It's Not the End of the World *by Judy Blume.*

Independent Reading in the Age of Common Core © 2013 by Sue Cannone-Calick & Elizabeth Henley • Scholastic Teaching Resources

VISUALIZING

Like the previous mini-lesson focus on Text-to-Self Connections, this strategy is a student favorite because it's accessible to all readers. SmartNoting here requires readers to use their five senses to fully experience a text. Writing down what they see, feel, hear, smell, and taste is empowering because students realize they understand what is happening. When reading informational texts, students are often exposed to unfamiliar material, so visualizing is a great strategy to "see" what the author is presenting.

Visualizing SmartNotes Mini-Lesson for Fiction

(CCSS) **RL.5.4, RL.6.4, RL.7.4, RL.8.4**

> **MATERIALS**
> • Mentor text: *Catherine, Called Birdy* by Karen Cushman (teacher copy and one copy for each student)
> • Chart paper and markers or whiteboard (dry-erase or interactive) with markers
> • Student notebooks and pencils

STEP 1 Explain the purpose of instruction.

Visualizing is an extremely accessible strategy. When we ask students to make a picture in their heads, we are expecting them to use all their senses to imagine the scene the author is creating. We want them to really visualize (experience) what the author is describing in order to better understand the text.

(At this point, the class is on page 160 of the book, and students have done some visualizing and thinking about historical fiction.)

Sue: As we continue exploring the Middle Ages and reading *Catherine, Called Birdy*, it is important that we all keep in mind how very different the world was back then. We need to remember how different life was so we can understand the choices Catherine makes. Getting a picture in your head of 1290 England is what we are going to continue to work on today.

STEP 2 Demonstrate the strategy in action.

(Sue turns to page 160 in the text and asks students to do so, too.)

Sue: When we stopped reading yesterday, Catherine, her father, and Morwenna were going to Lincoln to the tooth puller—oh dear, this sounds painful. Catherine is excited to go and see more of the world. What do we know about the world she lives in? Listen as I read the next two paragraphs. I am going to try to get a picture in my head—you do the same.

(Sue reads a description of the city, and students follow along. Then she stops on page 162.)

Sue: Wow—reading Cushman's words, I could imagine a bustling city. What a contrast from Catherine's manor house. Now I think I understand why she was excited to go—she can see what life is like outside the walls of her house. I want to write a Visualizing SmartNote about this quote:

"The crowded city swarmed with dogs, cats, roosters, geese, pigs, horses, merchants, travelers, housewives hurrying to market, children running with their buckets to the well, serving maids emptying chamber pots, and all manner of busy, bustling creatures . . . while another gathered them up in her apron and hurried off to make soup." (p. 161)

Please copy it in your notebook.

STEP 3 Interact with the text.

Sue: What did you visualize as I read this quote?

Noelle: I can't believe stealing spoiled fish was a crime! And they threw rotten vegetables at the thief!

Gaby: I can't believe an old woman picked up the rotten vegetables and made soup!

Sue: What does this picture help you understand about the Middle Ages?

Gaby: Life was different for some people, like people threw away rotten vegetables and others needed them to eat, so there is a big difference between rich and poor people.

Jordan: Oh, and Catherine only gets the best of everything, and is not happy about it.

Sue: The picture I am getting of the Middle Ages is that it was a busy, messy, loud time where some people have a lot, and others get by any way they can. Let's add this to our SmartNote:

Life was different for some people, like people threw away rotten vegetables and others needed them to eat, so there is a big difference between rich and poor people. Catherine only gets the best of everything and is not happy about it. The Middle Ages was a busy, messy, loud time where some people have a lot, and others get by any way they can.

STEP 4 Practice through independent reading

(After students add this thinking to their SmartNote, Sue transitions into independent reading practice.)

Sue: Great thinking today! As you return to your independent reading books, remember to keep a picture in your head of the scene the author is describing. Visualizing should help you understand the text better. At the end of independent reading, some of you will share. I am coming around for conferences as you read.

(Students start to read, and Sue begins her first conference.)

STEP 5 Share.

(After ten minutes, Sue calls the class together.)

Sue: Who wants to share what they *saw* today!

Jacob: I'm reading *The Forest of Hands and Teeth*, and I got a picture in my head of what the others looked like—gross and scary!

Sue: How did that help you understand the story better?

Jacob: Now I really know why the citizens are so scared—and desperate to run away.

Sue: The pictures you create really show that you are understanding your texts.

VISUALIZING SMARTNOTE SAMPLES

Dear Ms. Cannone,

One scene that I was able to visualize in <u>A Taste of Danger</u> was when Nancy realized that "Monica Sanchez" was really Sylvia Green, a food critic in disguise. The sentence that really helped me visualize the scene was "perched at a cocky angle, on a Styrofoam mannequin head, was Monica's gloriously thick hair. A wig!" It was helpful to visualize this scene because once the book said that, I knew something was phony about her. It also was important to visualize the scene because it helped me understand the book better.

Excellent

Leviathian

10-14-11 pg. 1 "A zeppelin scouted no-mans-land at the center of the battlefield, its metal skin sparkling." I can see a cannon aimed at the middle of a war battlefield, but what's weird is their walking. This is important because it could change what's going on in the war.

pg. 8 "A cannon was mounted in its belly, and the stubby noses of two Spandau sprouted from its head, which was as big as a smokehouse". I can see a huge war robot standing in someones backyard. This is important because Alek's never worked a war machine loaded with ammo before so he's scared.

Peculiar Chidren 9/23/11

✓① Page 35 "... I'd be sure that nearby, lurking in a stand of dark trees, beyond the next car in a parking lot, behind the garage where I kept my bike, it was waiting"

I see a dark figure with moon like eyes just stalking this house in little nooks or in the shadows

· Perhaps the monster will try to strike

9/26/11

GRADE 5:

(top left) Jessica, immersed in the Nancy Drew series, is reading A Taste of Danger and reflects on Carolyn Keene's word choice and visualized the scene.

GRADE 6:

(tope right) Gaby is reading Leviathan by Scott Westerfeld. He visualizes a battle scene and records why he thought these pictures are important.

(bottom right) As Nick reads Miss Peregrine's Home for Peculiar Children by Ransom Riggs, he uses the picture he creates in his head to predict an events in the plot.

MINI-LESSON

Visualizing SmartNotes Mini-Lesson for Nonfiction

CCSS RI.5.4, RI.5.5, RI.6.4, RI.6.5, RI.7.4, RI.7.5, RI.8.4, RI.8.5

MATERIALS
- Mentor text: Excerpts from *Chasing Lincoln's Killer* by James L. Swanson (teacher copy and one copy for each student)
- Chart paper and markers or whiteboard (dry-erase or interactive) with markers
- Student notebooks and pencils

STEP 1 **Explain the purpose of instruction.**

Visualizing is a useful strategy to use to tackle nonfiction. By creating a picture, using all five senses, readers can make sense of complex texts and ideas. When dealing with unfamiliar subjects and their terminology, visualizing can be particularly helpful.

(Sue displays the mentor text excerpt and distributes a copy to each student.)

Sue: We have been talking a lot about how to read and understand nonfiction. Today, we will focus on using visualizing, a strategy you know well, to help you do this. The text we will use is this excerpt from *Chasing Lincoln's Killer* by James L. Swanson. Since many of us don't know all the details about Lincoln's assassination, and none of us were alive then, picturing the information will be a useful strategy for us to use to fully understand this text.

STEP 2 Demonstrate the strategy in action.

Sue: This has been my independent reading book for the past week. I chose it because I never knew all the details behind this story. Last night I got past the part where Lincoln was killed and started reading about the manhunt for his killer. Everyone was looking for John Wilkes Booth and his accomplices. This part was really exciting, and I had to visualize the scene to keep track of all the events. Listen as I read you this short passage. I will think aloud and share my visualizing.

Let me give you a little background before I read: Booth has just shot the president, jumped down from the balcony, and broken his leg. As a reader, I assumed that this would make him easy to apprehend, but I was wrong. Eventually, it takes the government twelve days to find him.

(Sue reads aloud page 74 and then stops.)

Sue: I relied on my senses to really understand what was happening. First, I knew it was dark. Swanson writes, "nightfall had obscured the hills." Next, I knew Booth was nervous: "he heard a noise in the distance: horses' hooves pounding the earth." He thought it was the whole cavalry after him. I didn't feel bad for him, but I could imagine that the idea of getting caught was making him anxious. Lastly, I remembered Booth had a broken leg, so I could imagine the pain he was dealing with. Let's record this in a SmartNote:

"nightfall had obscured the hills" (p. 74) *I was able to picture that it was dark, which must have added to his nervousness,* given that Booth "heard a noise in the distance: horses' hooves." (p. 74) *He thought he was about to get caught.*

STEP 3 Interact with the text.

(Sue displays the second excerpt and gives a copy to each student.)

Sue: I am now going to put another excerpt on the board, and this time, you are going to practice using visualizing to fully understand the text. This passage occurs while Booth and his accomplice are hiding in a pine thicket in Maryland, waiting to escape to Virginia. Follow along while I read aloud to you from page 137.

(Sue reads aloud and then gives students time to think.)

Sue: What were you able to visualize?

Devon: I pictured two dirty, smelly men.

Sue: Yes, given that Swanson says that, it is a good thing to note.

Chris: I liked the part where he writes that they were "wearing the equivalent of a modern day business suit."

Sue: Why?

Chris: I liked the words.

Independent Reading in the Age of Common Core © 2013 by Sue Cannone-Calick & Elizabeth Henley • Scholastic Teaching Resources

Sue: Good, but what did you picture—those words can help you make a picture.

Marissa: My dad wears a suit to work; I can't imagine him camping in it.

Sue: Good point. A suit is not appropriate for camping. What did the picture help you understand?

Devon: Oh, I get it. I saw a man wearing a suit, but it's all dirty now. He is not dressed for being outside.

Sue: He certainly can't be comfortable, but even worse . . . what would happen if he were seen?

Marissa: He would be very noticeable looking the way he does.

Sue: Yes, exactly. Booth wasn't comfortable, but he couldn't step out of the thicket because he would catch attention and be captured. Visualizing the scene helped you do more than just picture Swanson's words—it helped you understand Booth's situation and the plot of the book. Let's write this down in our SmartNote:

 "He left Washington wearing the equivalent of a modern day business suit. . . . He and Herrold could not bathe or wash clothes and, unshaven, they looked and smelled worse each day." (p. 137) *He would be very noticeable looking the way he does, and wouldn't be able to leave his hiding spot for fear of being caught.*

STEP 4 Practice through independent reading.

(Sue waits for students to finish copying the SmartNote she's written on the board.)

Sue: In a moment, I am going to ask you to start reading your independent nonfiction book. Please practice visualizing. If you take a really strong visualizing SmartNote, please share it with us at the end.

(Students read independently while Sue and Betsy have one-on-one conferences.)

STEP 5 Share.

Sue: When I met with Sasha, she got a great picture in her head. Sasha, please share your thinking.

Sasha: I'm reading *Blizzard* by Jim Murphy. When Ms. Cannone came over, I had just read about a girl named Sarah who was in a train that crashed during the blizzard. The passengers were forced to get off the train and walk, and Sarah got separated from the group.

Sue: Where did visualizing help you?

Sasha: Here is the part: "At some point, Sarah ran out of strength entirely and stopped moving. Snow and ice clung to her clothes, hair and face as if she were a statue in a park. Then the icy figure toppled over backward. Her will to struggle, to push herself up and keep moving, was gone. She lay there as if she were on the softest of featherbeds." (p. 24) *I saw just how powerful this storm was that it threw a train off its track and basically killed this girl. I can see how she just drifted off into the soft snow.*

Sue: Wow—that is powerful. The author, Jim Murphy, really helped readers imagine this scene. Thank you.

Claudia: Wait, do you have another copy of that book, Ms. Cannone? I want to read it too.

Sue: I think I might, let's go look.

QUESTIONING

What strategy is next? And why? Good questions! In the Questioning mini-lesson, SmartNoters learn to pay attention to what they are wondering about when they read. Although many readers will ask questions that will have ready answers in the text, we encourage them to ask open-ended questions for which they will have to work to answer. Asking questions while reading nonfiction texts is crucial. Questions show student engagement—all the more important when reading new information.

Questioning SmartNotes
Mini-Lesson for Fiction

RL.5.5, RL.5.6, RL.6.5, RL.6.6, RL.7.5, RL.7.6, RL.8.5, RL.8.6

> **MATERIALS**
> • Mentor text: *Walk Two Moons* by Sharon Creech (teacher copy and one copy for each student)
> • Chart paper and markers or whiteboard (dry-erase or interactive) with markers
> • Student notebooks and pencils

STEP 1 **Explain the purpose of instruction.**

Asking good questions is the mark of a strong reader. Wondering and writing down these musings in a SmartNote is important. Questioning encourages a reader to read on and to clarify points of confusion. Asking questions is proof of thinking.

(Sue moves into the second day of a mini-lesson on questioning.)

Sue: Yesterday we read chapter 1 of *Walk Two Moons*. We wrote lots of questions in our SmartNotes; let's go back and look at them:

Why did she move to Euclid, Ohio?

Who is "I" (Is it Sal?)

Did she really leave something in the back of her closet? Why?

What peculiar things will happen to Phoebe Winterbottom?

Why is she locked in her car with her grandparents for six days?

How are Sal's and Phoebe's stories connected?

It's smart that you all had these questions. Sharon Creech started her book this way to make you wonder and want to read on. When you record your questions in SmartNotes like we did, it's good because you see what you wondered about and you have a place to record answers. These questions will help us as we read on. Some of them are questions we will get answers to quickly; others will take some time to answer but they are important, too. Readers are supposed to wonder while they read. Smart readers always do this.

 Independent Reading in the Age of Common Core © 2013 by Sue Cannone-Calick & Elizabeth Henley • Scholastic Teaching Resources

STEP 2 Demonstrate the strategy in action.

(Sue begins to read chapter 2 aloud but stops at the end of the first paragraph.)

Sue: Wait a second, I'm confused. On page four, I just read, "It was after all the adventures of Phoebe that my grandparents came up with a plan to drive from Kentucky to Ohio, where they would pick me up, and then the three of us would drive two thousand miles west to Lewiston, Idaho." At the end of chapter one, Sal had just arrived in Ohio. Why is she leaving again? Sometimes, when I am confused, rereading helps. Let me try that.

(Sue reads the first sentence aloud again, emphasizing "It was after.")

Okay, now I think I may understand. Creech is going to fill us in—but she is telling us that this already happened. Sal already took the trip with her grandparents, and Phoebe already had her adventures. Creech is starting at the end of the story, and then jumping back to the beginning to fill us in. As readers, we need to pay attention to our confusion/wonderings so we can figure things out. You need to write down your questions, and think them out. Ignoring your questions will make you confused. Let's take a SmartNote:

"It was after all the adventures of Phoebe that my grandparents came up with a plan to drive from Kentucky to Ohio, where they would pick me up, and then the three of us would drive two thousand miles west to Lewiston, Idaho." (p. 4) *Sal already took the trip with her grandparents, and Phoebe already had her adventures. Sharon Creech is starting at the end, and then jumping back to the beginning to fill us in."*

(Students copy the SmartNote into their notebooks.)

STEP 3 Interact with the text.

(Then Sue continues to read chapter 2 aloud.)

Sue: Let's stop reading, here at the end of page five, when Sal lists the real reasons she took the trip. Read them to yourself again, and we will write some Question SmartNotes.

(Sue gives students time to read this section.)

Sue: What are you wondering about?

Taylor: Why is Sal afraid to see her momma?

Mike: Why didn't Sal's dad take her when he saw Momma?

Sarah: What does "resting peacefully" mean?

Sue: These questions are really thoughtful. We know this because their answers will matter to the story. They will help us understand Sal, and her trip. We probably won't get answers to these questions right away, but keep them in mind and refer back to them as we learn answers. We will come back to this page of SmartNotes when we find answers.

(Sue records the text from page five and students' questions in SmartNote form, and students copy them into their notebooks as shown below.)

1. "Gram and Gramps wanted to see Momma, who was resting peacefully in Lewiston, Idaho."

2. "Gram and Gramps knew that I wanted to see Momma, but that I was afraid to."

3. "Dad wanted to be alone with the red-headed Margaret Cadaver. He had already seen Momma, and he had not taken me." (p. 5)

Why is Sal afraid to see her momma?

Why didn't Sal's dad take her when he saw Momma?

What does "resting peacefully" mean?

STEP 4 Practice through independent reading.

Sue: Okay, as you read your independent reading book, we want you to pay attention to the questions you have. When you are confused, or just wondering something, create a SmartNote for that question. Add the text that prompted the question. I will come around to have conferences with some of you, and at the end of class, you will share some of your thinking.

STEP 5 Share.

(Sue calls the class together.)

Sue: Who would like to share a question they had that they thought was important?

Rick: I am reading *Holes* by Louis Sachar, and sometimes I get confused when the author jumps around in time. My question was: What does Madame Zeroni have to do with the rest of the story?

Sue: Very thoughtful question—the answer will be important—good job.

QUESTIONING SMARTNOTE SAMPLES

Below are a number of Question SmartNotes samples ranging from the more literal to the inferential. The important part of a Question SmartNote is that it pushes the reader to think about the answer as reading continues.

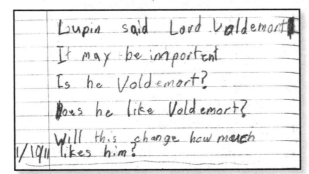

Lupin said Lord Voldemort
It may be important
Is he Voldemort?
Does he like Voldemort?
Will this change how much
1/19/11 likes him?

②"The Carnival should be spectacular. I can't wait to find out what our work assignments will be."
what — what carnival?—why is "Carnival" capitalized?
work assignments?
why?

GRADE 5:

Sam, reading Harry Potter and the Prisoner of Azkaban *by J. K. Rowling, asks large and literal questions that are likely to be answered over the course of the novel.*

Jessica is in the midst of reading all the Nancy Drew mysteries by Carolyn Keene and asks specific questions about one book's plot and setting. Again, these questions help Jessica make sense of the text.

P.28 "Hairpins," Mrs. Bidsom said with a smile. "If you put your hair up, you'll look older."
I don't really ~~understand~~ need to this quote.
well why does she look older?
If she is not doing it for money, and just to school the kids, then why does she need to do that?

"Luv Ya Bunches" By: Lauren Myracle 11/8/
① When I read, "It's easier to be one of the Populars, that's all." (143). I had a question. why did she think that? Does she think it's easier to be followed by others than to follow others?

GRADE 6:

As Giana reads The Secret School *by Avi, she reflects on a character and her motivation.*

Heenal is reading Luv Ya Bunches *by Lauren Myracle. She uses her questions to reflect on social issues in middle school.*

Independent Reading in the Age of Common Core © 2013 by Sue Cannone-Calick & Elizabeth Henley • Scholastic Teaching Resources

CLARIFYING CONFUSION

Informational text often presents vocabulary challenges for readers. Students stumble over words they don't know. Ignoring these words will lead to confusion. Asking good questions clarifies confusion for readers. It helps students focus their thinking on the information they are learning; in many cases with nonfiction reading, this is related to vocabulary.

Clarifying Confusion SmartNote Mini-Lesson for Nonfiction

(CCSS) RI.5.4, L.5.4, RI.6.4, L.6.4, RI.7.4, L.7.4, RI.8.4, L.8.4

> **MATERIALS**
> • Mentor text: *Amelia Lost: The Life and Disappearance of Amelia Earhart* by Candace Fleming (teacher copy and one copy for each student)
> • Chart paper and markers or whiteboard (dry-erase or interactive) with markers
> • Student notebooks and pencils

STEP 1 **Explain the purpose of instruction.**

This lesson teaches students strategies for managing unfamiliar words that often pop up in informational text. Although some texts will boldface technical terms or have glossaries or vocabulary boxes, readers need to be confident in using context clue strategies.

(Sue displays the mentor text excerpt, and distributes a copy to each student.)

Sue: We have been talking a lot about how to read and understand nonfiction. Today, we will focus on asking good questions that will help us understand informational text. Our text is an excerpt from *Amelia Lost: The Life and Disappearance of Amelia Earhart* by Candace Fleming. Since many of us don't know about Amelia Earhart, and many of us don't know much about airplanes, we can anticipate encountering unknown vocabulary—and we can't just skip over it. Asking questions and thinking through the text is important to make sense of unknown words.

STEP 2 **Demonstrate the strategy in action.**

Sue: I'm going to read an excerpt from the text. This portion is technical, but we can't just ignore that specific vocabulary—the author wouldn't have used it if it wasn't important. Our job is to use the information in the text to make our best guesses about unfamiliar words. I'm going to start a SmartNote to help us figure out the vocabulary. (Sue reads and then records the passage below.)

"They both believed so, and George flung himself into the preparations. He hired aeronautical experts, who added extra fuel tanks to both wings, and the cabin of the Vega. They strengthened the fuselage with braces so it could support the increased weight of the added fuel." (p. 72)

Sue: This paragraph has a lot of technical words in it. I know it's about airplanes, but these words (Sue underlines the words as she says them)—*aeronautical* and *fuselage*—I don't know what they mean. Should I skip them?

Students: No!

Sue: I was joking. There are strategies to figure these words out—and skipping them is never a good idea. When unfamiliar words prevent me from fully understanding what is going on in a text, I stop, reread, and try to make a picture in my head. I picture . . . a plane, with big fuel tanks, and thick wires. With that picture, I then try to use other words in the place of the challenging vocabulary. If I can do that, I am pretty sure I understand what is going on. Let me try to figure out what *aeronautical* means. "He hired aeronautical experts, who added extra fuel tanks to both wings." *Aeronautical* is a word describing the expert. I think the expert here must be a plane expert because he or she knows how to do this. *Aeronautical* is a word having to do with planes.

STEP 3 Interact with the text.

Sue: Now let's try the same strategy for *fuselage*. "They strengthened the fuselage with braces so it could support the increased weight of the added fuel." What word could fit here?

Jen: I think the word *plane* would fit. It would make sense, too, because with the extra weight, the whole plane would need to be stronger.

Sue: Bravo. Let's write a SmartNote to keep track of our thinking around these new words:

"He hired aeronautical experts, who added extra fuel tanks to both wings." (p. 72) *Aeronautical is a word describing the expert. I think the expert here must be a plane expert because he or she knows how to do this. Aeronautical is a word having to do with planes.*

"They strengthened the fuselage with braces so it could support the increased weight of the added fuel." (p. 72) *What word could fit here? I think the word plane would fit. It would make sense, too, because with the extra weight, the whole plane would need to be stronger.*

STEP 4 Practice through independent reading.

Sue: When you return to your nonfiction books for independent reading, focus your SmartNote on unfamiliar words—no skipping over them!

(Sue and Betsy have conferences while students read for ten minutes.)

STEP 5 Share.

Sue: As Ms. Henley and I were conferring, I met with Megan, and Megan, I'd like you to share what you did today. Everyone should learn the strategy you used.

Megan: I'm reading *Ten True Tales: Surviving Sharks and Other Dangerous Creatures*, I read about a wolf, and the text said, "holding out half a sandwich in an attempt to coax a grey wolf to come closer." (p. 62). Then I wrote: *What's coax?* I got a picture in my head and tried to use the fill-in-the-blank strategy, but I couldn't do it. You told me to read on, and I did.

Sue: Great, read the text that helped you.

Megan: (reads) "holding out half a sandwich in an attempt to coax a grey wolf to come closer. 'C'mon, boy. I'm not gonna hurt ya,' the trucker said in a high pitched tone." Now, I could guess that *coax* meant something like trying to get him to come over.

Sue: Yes, you are right, *coax* means "to tempt"; does that fit in the story?

Megan: Awesome. Yes.

Sue: Add your good thinking to your SmartNote.

PREDICTING

If you think a mini-lesson on Predicting SmartNotes will come next, you are correct! This is taught after the Questioning mini-lesson because after thinking about a question, it makes sense to use knowledge of the text to make an educated guess about the plot. Wild predictions must be avoided; worthwhile guesses take into consideration previously learned information—they are thoughtful and text based. For this reason, Predicting SmartNotes are not effective when reading informational text.

Predicting SmartNotes Mini-Lesson for Fiction

(CCSS) RL.5.3, RL.5.5, RL.6.3, RL.6.5, RL.7.3, RL.7.5, RL.8.3, RL.8.5

> ### MATERIALS
> - Mentor text: *Walk Two Moons* by Sharon Creech (teacher copy and one copy for each student)
> - Chart paper and markers or whiteboard (dry-erase or interactive) with markers
> - Student notebooks and pencils

STEP 1 Explain the purpose of instruction.

It's sensible for readers to make predictions after they have asked questions. The predictions should be based on what has occurred in the text.

Betsy: You're really good now about noticing when you wonder about something when you read. We are ready to move on now to making strong predictions. When you make a prediction, you use what you know from the story to guess at what will happen next or what the character will do next. Wild, crazy predictions are not allowed. They are silly, but more important, they do not help you as a reader. When readers use what they know to guess what will happen next, this shows that they understand the story and can think ahead. Making SmartNotes about your predictions is a way to keep track of your predictions and check if they are accurate.

STEP 2 Demonstrate the strategy in action.

Betsy: I'm going to start reading chapter three in *Walk Two Moons*, and I will stop when I'm ready to make a prediction.

(Betsy starts reading aloud chapter three and stops at page 10.)

Betsy: On page ten Sal said, "Who cares how he met Margaret Cadaver?" I wondered how the two met and why Sal doesn't seem to care. I am going to write the quote and my question as a SmartNote. When I learn more, maybe I can make a prediction:

"Who cares how he met Margaret Cadaver?" (p. 10) *How did they meet? Why doesn't Sal want to know?*

(Betsy continues to read and then stops on page 13.)

Betsy: It seems that Sal and her dad are spending lots of time at Margaret's house. Because they are eating there so often, and the fact that we learned earlier that Sal doesn't want to know how they met, I predict that Sal's dad and Margaret will date.

(Betsy records the SmartNote below, and students copy it into their notebooks.)

"We ate dinner there three times that week." (p. 13) *Because they are eating there so often, and the fact that we learned earlier that Sal doesn't want to know how they met, I predict that Sal's dad and Margaret will date.*

(**NB:** This is an inaccurate prediction. Betsy knows this, but Creech's hints are credible and lead readers to think a lot about the relationships of these three characters, and that is important. When students realize that the prediction is wrong—it is such an aha! moment—it enforces the power of predicting and validating predictions.)

STEP **3** Interact with the text.

Betsy: Keep in mind, that asking good questions when you read can lead to your making strong predictions. Let's keep reading.

(Betsy finishes reading the chapter.)

Betsy: Now that we have finished the chapter, I notice that most of it was Creech filling in background information. This is valuable, even though we didn't learn more about Sal's journey or her friendship with Phoebe. Authors don't waste space, so make a prediction about how this background information might be useful.

Olivia: In this chapter, we meet the kids in Sal's class. Maybe they will be important later on.

Jack: Oh, Sal's other grandparents are also mentioned; maybe they will be important later, too.

Betsy: You got it. Like I said before, authors don't waste space. They give you information you will need at different times, leaving you, the reader, to think about what they wrote. Then let's SmartNote those predictions so we can come back to them later:
Chapter 3: I predict Sal's friends will be important later on. I also predict that Sal's other grandparents will be in the story later on, too.

STEP **4** Practice through independent reading.

Betsy: As you read independently today, keep asking good questions, and SmartNote them. When you can, use the information you have read to make a solid prediction. After reading today, some of you will share your predictions.

(As students read and take SmartNotes, Betsy and Sue confer with several students.)

STEP **5** Share.

(Based on her conferences, Betsy calls on Lisa to share.)

Betsy: I predict that Lisa wants to share!

Lisa (smiling): Okay, I'm reading *Charlotte's Web*, and I love it. One question I had was if Charlotte was going to be able to save Wilbur. I predicted that she would.

Betsy: What information in the text helped you make that prediction?

Lisa: Charlotte is smart and is a good friend to Wilbur. I think her good ideas could save him.

PREDICTING SMARTNOTES SAMPLES

> [17 Santa gave
>
> Mrs. B - sewing machine
> Mr. B - a finished drum
> Peter - Shield and Sword
> Susan - bow and arrow
> Lucy - dagger and potion (healing)
> This will be good for battle
> fore shoulds

> p.59 Joey talks back to people (Mrs. Maxy)
>
> p.61 Joey eats Dunkin Donuts
>
> p.67 "Mrs. Maxy had a conference in the morning so our class had a substitute named Miss Adams."
>
> I think Joey is going to be rude to miss Adams because he talks rude to other teachers

> p.12 WIR "Hail, Emperor, those about to die salute you" I thought this was odd because they would never salute him again. If they survived through the battle how were they going to die? Through animals, through knifes?
>
> p.17 WIR "Perhaps life would be better there," I predicted that life will be better there. I thought this because since Rome was having political problems, and nobody was safe, I think that Athens their hometown, will be better. It is just so astounding that some people never lose hope, and never think, it will be okay here. They think they will have a better life over there.

GRADE 5:

(top left) Sam is still reading The Lion, the Witch, and the Wardrobe *by C. S. Lewis. He lists information he's learned and uses it to make a prediction that is rooted in the text.*

(top right) Henry is reading Joey Pigza Loses Control *by Jack Gantos and uses his knowledge of Joey to predict future behavior.*

(bottom right) Reading the Atticus of Rome *by Barry Denenberg, Geoffrey again uses background knowledge—this time to predict the quality of life in Athens.*

TEXT-TO-TEXT CONNECTIONS

Readers make text-to-text connections when they note similarities between texts they know. Noticing connections (similar characters, settings, conflicts, themes, or authors' styles) helps readers get a fuller understanding of the text in front of them. Moreover, text-to-text connections can help readers visualize more clearly or understand character, plot, and setting.

Text-to-Text Connections SmartNotes Mini-Lesson for Fiction

(CCSS) **RL.5.9, RL.6.9, RL.7.9, RL.8.9**

MATERIALS
- Mentor texts: *Hatchet* by Gary Paulsen and *Sign of the Beaver* by Elizabeth George Speare (teacher copy and one copy for each student)
- Chart paper and markers or whiteboard (dry-erase or interactive) with markers
- Student notebooks and pencils

STEP 1 Explain the purpose of the instruction.

After this lesson, students will know how noticing and recording similarities between texts help them understand each text at a deeper level.

Sue: Readers recognize similarities between books. Sometimes, we may see a similarity in characters, problems, settings, or feelings. Using information from one text could help you understand another text. Noticing these similarities and writing them down not only shows how wise you are, but it also makes reading fun.

STEP 2 Demonstrate strategy in action.

(This is the second day of reading *Sign of the Beaver*.)

Sue: Yesterday, we started reading *Sign of the Beaver*. Almost immediately, this book made me think of another story I have read. Did any of you notice a similarity to another text?

Helen: Oh yeah, *Hatchet*.

(There are shouts of agreement from the rest of the class.)

Sue: Yes, good job. There are similarities between *Sign of the Beaver* and *Hatchet*, even though *Sign of the Beaver* was written about a different time period than *Hatchet*. Right away, after reading the first page, we know that Matt is alone in the wilderness. I'm going to write a quote from this page on the board. Please copy it in your notebooks, too:

"In the summer his father would go back to Massachusetts to fetch his mother and sister and new baby, who would be born while they were gone. Matt would stay behind and guard the cabin and the corn patch." (p. 2)

Now, we have to add our thinking to this quote to make it a SmartNote. When I read it, I thought, *Huh, Matt is alone just like Brian was alone in the wilderness. They are alone for different reasons, but still alone. I wonder if they will face similar problems?*

(Sue adds this thought to the quote, and students record it in their notebook.)

This text-to-text connection was about the settings of the two books. It led us to a question about plot. Connections can be about anything that is related to the text. Using these connections to help us understand both texts better is the key. Let's keep reading, and pay attention to any similarities we can make between the two books.

STEP 3 Interact with the text.

(Sue begins to read chapter 2 aloud with students following along. She stops on page 8.)

Sue: Here we are on page eight, not far into the chapter, but we need to talk and think. Did anyone notice a similarity to *Hatchet* as I read?

Frankie: We just read that Matt's job is to take care of the corn patch, and that is hard work.

Sue: How does that connect to *Hatchet*?

Frankie: Brian also had to work hard.

Sue: Try to be more specific here, Frankie. Everyone think back to *Hatchet*. Why did Brian have to work hard?

(Sue provides about three minutes of wait time for her students to think.)

Frankie: He worked hard to get the fire, and then to keep it going.

Independent Reading in the Age of Common Core © 2013 by Sue Cannone-Calick & Elizabeth Henley • Scholastic Teaching Resources

Sue: Exactly. Let's write this SmartNote down:

"The corn patch needed constant tending." (p. 8) *Like Brian who had to work hard to tend his fire, Matt has to work hard to keep up with the corn patch.*

Making the connection that both boys work hard is important, but there is more thinking to be done. How will this connection help you as a reader? Does it help you visualize, predict, infer, ask questions?

(Sue lets the question linger until she gets a response.)

Brandon: I can picture two boys in the woods working hard.

Sue: Good. Anyone else?

Julie: I wonder if a moose will attack Matt like Brian was attacked.

Nick: What about if a porcupine attacks, too?

(The class giggles.)

Sue: Yes, Brian did face many hardships in *Hatchet*, and in *Sign of the Beaver* Matt might suffer some, too. But let's not get silly; keep your predictions based on the text and important details. Brian and Matt are in the woods alone: they are both left to survive. Because we know that Brian managed to survive, with bumps along the way, we anticipate that Matt will, too—despite problems (like the porcupine and the moose) that may pop up. We used this text-to-text connection to make a reasonable prediction. Let's add our prediction to the end of the SmartNote:

Brian faced many problems but he made it. I think that Matt will also face many problems but that he will survive, too.

STEP **4** Practice through independent reading.

Sue: When you read your independent book today, pay attention to any text-to-text connections you can make. Don't forget to think about how the connection helps you—we will share your SmartNotes at the end of the period.

(As students read independently and take SmartNotes, Sue and Betsy hold individual conferences.)

STEP **5** Share.

(Before the end of class, Sue brings the class together to share their work.)

Phyllis: I'm reading *Who Is Barack Obama?* and I learned that in 1959, there was something called Jim Crowe laws that kept black people apart from white people. Then I thought of the book *Number the Stars* by Lois Lowry. Jewish people during World War Two had to close down their shops.

Sue: Amazing connection. How does this thinking help you understand what you are reading in *Who Is Barack Obama*?

Phyllis: Well, I think that sometimes, things aren't right. People are mean.

Sue: You are right. Keep thinking about this injustice as you keep reading.

TEXT-TO-TEXT SMARTNOTES SAMPLES

Heenal, a sixth grader reading The Name of This Book Is Secret *by Pseudonymous Bosch, uses her connection to* The Mysterious Benedict Society *by Trenton Lee Stewart to reflect on character.*

> "The Name of this Book is Secret" 10/10/
> ① When I read," Cass is a survivalist"
> on p.12, I made a text to text
> connection. In another book I
> have read, the main character was
> also a survivalist and usually
> they carry around a backpack
> with lots of things. The book I am
> talking about is "The Mysterious
> Benedict Society" is which Kate, a main character
> carries around a bucket that holds
> emergency tools that could help her
> at any time. Some of these items
> include a rope and a flashlight,

MINI-LESSON

TEXT-TO-WORLD CONNECTIONS

Between all their independent reading, our class texts, and what students are exposed to in social studies, science, and math, they should be thinking about the world—society, media, culture. Students can use what they know (their background knowledge) to understand their reading, but they can also use what they learn through reading independently to think about human nature, the world, and current events.

Text-to-World Connections
SmartNotes Mini-Lesson for Fiction

(CCSS) **RL.5.6, RL.6.6, RL.7.6, RL.8.6**

> ### MATERIALS
> - Mentor text: *Flipped* by Wendelin Van Drannen (teacher copy and one copy for each student)
> - Chart paper and markers or whiteboard (dry-erase or interactive) with markers
> - Student notebooks and pencils

STEP 1 Explain the purpose of instruction.

Text-to-world connections require students to use what they know of the world to understand the characters and plot of the book they are reading. This strategy requires students to think outside their personal perimeter.

(Betsy continues a discussion of the novel *Flipped*, focusing on making text-to-world connections.)

Betsy: We have been reading about Julianna and Bryce and how hard it is for them to be friends. They have a hard time being honest about how they feel. I know that when people want someone to like them, they often do strange things, and aren't honest with themselves or other people. Do you know what I mean?

(Students nod.)

Betsy: When readers use what they know about the world, people, cultures, and/or human nature to understand what they are reading, this is called a text-to-world connection. This connection helps readers think beyond themselves.

STEP 2 Demonstrate the strategy in action.

(Betsy begins reading aloud and finishes Bryce's chapter—titled "Flipped.")

Betsy: The problem Bryce and Julianna are having right now rings so true to me. I've been in middle school, teach middle school, have watched TV shows about middle school kids, so I can imagine this scene. There's a quote on page 183 that made me think about how confusing and unsettling it is when you like someone.

(The class giggles, and a few faces turn red. Betsy writes the quote and her thinking on the whiteboard and asks students to record it in their notebooks.)

"I didn't care where I was, I didn't care who I saw. I wanted, just had to kiss her. I leaned in, closed my eyes, and then . . ." (p. 183) *This made me think about what I know about the world of middle school. It is confusing and unsettling when you like someone; it is hard to be honest. I can picture how mortifying the scene must have been for both of them.*

STEP 3 Interact with the text.

Betsy: Middle schoolers try really hard to impress one another—at times hurting others and not being honest.

(There are nods of agreement and some whispering.)

Betsy: Think back over what we have read. When did you think to yourself: *That rings true to what I know about the world of middle school.*

(Betsy gives students about three minutes of thinking time.)

Betsy: Now that you have that moment in your head, write a SmartNote. Find the quote and add your thinking.

(Betsy gives them eight minutes to do this, and she and Sue walk around to see what students are writing. They notice that Carly is eager to share.)

Betsy: Carly, what is your thinking?

Carly: When Bryce doesn't tell Julianna that he doesn't want her chicken eggs reminded me of middle school.

Betsy: Why? Explain. Tell us the quote and your thinking.

Carly: On page 79, it said, "And if he knew, how could he have been so heartless, just throwing my eggs away like that, week after week, year after year?" *Sometimes in middle school, boys and girls are embarrassed to tell the truth.*

(Betsy records Carly's quote and thinking on the board and asks students to copy it into their notebooks.)

Matt: Oh yeah, that was the first time Julianna actually cried.

Betsy: Making the text-to-world connection that kids have trouble being honest when they like each other, is great, but now you have to think about how this connection helps you understand the book better.

Matt: Oh . . . Bryce and Julianna have a very complicated relationship.

Betsy: And . . . how is this knowledge going to help you?

Carly: I think that they will be together at the end; I want them to be together at the end. I think they will because Bryce already was honest and tried to kiss her.

Matt: When I see boys and girls talking in the cafeteria—I wonder if they are really being honest.

Betsy: Me too!

STEP 4 Practice through independent reading.

Betsy: As you go to read independently, think about how the knowledge you have of the world could help you understand the book.

(As students read independently, we have individual conferences with two students each.)

STEP 5 Share.

(Betsy calls an end to independent reading and brings the class together to share.)

David: I'm reading *Monster* by Walter Dean Myers, and it's kind of the same as we were talking about before—teens aren't always honest. In this book, it's serious—the main character gets put in jail because of it.

TEXT-TO-WORLD SMARTNOTE SAMPLES

Geoffrey, a very bright sixth grader, uses his knowledge of immigrants to better understand Puck from The Scorpio Races *by Maggie Stiefvater. Geoffrey is an exceptional student, but all readers are capable of using knowledge of the world to help navigate their texts.*

MINI-LESSON

INFERRING

Students are now ready for inferential SmartNote thinking. The ability to make inferences is essential for truly deep understanding of a text. Inference SmartNotes require thinking beyond the text. In fiction, this might mean tapping into character traits, motivation, and change over time. With informational text, readers must use facts, figures, diagrams, charts, and illustrations to help them figure out what isn't being said explicitly.

Inferring SmartNotes Mini-Lesson for Fiction

(CCSS) RL.5.1, RL.6.1, RL.7.1, RL.8.1

> **MATERIALS**
> • Mentor text: *The Giver* by Lois Lowry (teacher copy and one copy for each student)
> • Chart paper and markers or whiteboard (dry-erase or interactive) with markers
> • Student notebooks and pencils

STEP 1 Explain the purpose of instruction.

Inferences are an important reading strategy, which must be taught, practiced, and retaught multiple times. When students infer, they read between the lines; they figure out what the author is implying instead of explicitly stating. Inferring is the work readers do to fully understand the text. It is a way for readers to be involved in and thinking through a text. All higher order thinking strategies are built on inferring.

(The class has read the first two chapters of *The Giver* together.)

Sue: We have been reading *The Giver* by Lois Lowry, and we have been noticing just how different this community is from ours. In that community, spouses and jobs are chosen for you, and there is no personal decision making. Lois Lowry has told us about the community Jonas lives in, but it is up to us to make sense of the place. This type of thinking is known as making inferences.

STEP 2 Demonstrate the strategy in action.

Sue: Let's look at yesterday's Summary SmartNote for all of chapter 2:

Ceremony for the Ones is when the family unit receives a child and the child is named. All children are allowed bicycles at the Nine's Ceremony. The Ceremony of Twelve was the last of the Ceremonies and the most important because kids got their Assignments.

This brief summary we took at the end of chapter two gives us a lot to think about. Let me share my thinking: This community is really structured—it has a lot of rules. The kids get the same things at the same time. Our world isn't like that. Lois Lowry never says that the community is structured, but I read between the lines and figured that out—that is called making an inference. Docs my thinking make sense? Someone explain this inference in your own words.

Tina: The inference is that Jonas's world is strict. Kids can't get bikes before they are nine; I got a bike when I was five—that stinks for them.

Sue: Exactly! Tina, your inference was based exactly from the text—and you added your own thoughts—great inference. Let's add this inference to our Summary SmartNote. Be sure you add it to your Summary SmartNote in your notebooks: *I can infer that this community is really structured, and strict. It has a lot of rules. I think this because all kids get the same things at the same time—our world isn't like that.*

STEP 3 Interact with the text.

Sue: Let's keep reading and make some more inferences.

(Sue starts reading chapter 3; students follow along in their books.)

Will: Wait, stop. I have a question. On page twenty you just read, "Almost every citizen in the community had dark eyes." Is that even possible? (Student independent thinking is encouraged during our reading of the class text. We are pleased by relevant student contributions.)

Sue: Great question. I don't know. Let's think about what the text tells us and see if we can figure it out, or make an inference about this.

Jonathan: We know that Jonas, the new baby, and a girl have pale eyes.

Sue: You are all noticing that it is not typical for so many people to have the same eye color. Let's keep reading, and maybe we will learn more. (Sue keeps reading, but suddenly stops at the top of page 21.)

Sue: We just got more information. Let's write this quote in our SmartNote: "Lily teased, 'maybe he had the same Birthmother as you.' Jonas followed them inside. . . . Mirrors were rare in the community; they weren't forbidden, but there was no real need of them." (p. 21) Based on this information, what can you figure out or infer? Let's try to make sense of this.

Nick: This community is messed up. Everything is controlled, everyone looks the same, so it is strange that Jonas and only a few others have pale eyes. No wonder they don't need mirrors.

Sue: Fabulous! You have actually made a number of inferences here. Lowry didn't tell us that everyone looks the same—you figured that out. Also, she didn't tell us that everything is controlled, but we have been collecting evidence about that. Let's all add these great inferences to the quote in our SmartNote:

Everything is controlled, everyone looks the same, so it is strange that Jonas and only a few others have pale eyes. No wonder they don't need mirrors.

STEP 4 Practice through independent reading.

(After students copy the SmartNote in their notebooks, Sue transitions to independent practice.)

Sue: Making inferences is all about making sense of the text and figuring things out. If you realize something that the author hasn't told you, you've made an inference. As you read your independent reading book, pay attention to the inferences you make, and be sure to add a quote from the text to show what inspired you to think between the lines.

STEP 5 Share.

(After ten minutes, Sue gathers the class together.)

Sue: Who wants to share an inference?

Mike: I'm reading *Eragon*, and I inferred that Eragon loves Saphira, his dragon.

Sue: Is there a place in the story where Eragon tells Saphira he loves her?

Mike: No, I figured it out!

Sue: What helped you figure this out?

Mike: The way he acts around her.

Sue: Be sure you have the actual words from the text in your SmartNote.

Mike: No problem.

Sue: Inferring is thinking; you will be doing a lot of it—get ready.

INFERRING SMARTNOTES SAMPLES

GRADE 5:

(top left) Harris is reading Zoobreak *by Gordon Korman and makes inferences about character traits.*

(top right) Cristina starts making a prediction, which leads to an inference, and eventually, a text-to text connection! She is reading The Name of this Book is Secret *by Pseudonymous Bosch.*

(bottom left) This is also Cristina's work. Later on in the year, while reading The Penderwicks *by Jeanne Birdsall, she makes a thoughtful inference about the relationships between characters.*

Zoobreak

12/3/11
p.37

Ben is	Mellisa is
smart	very very smart
determined	(Focused)
Brave	determined
(Focused)	silent
	Her room is filled with Super technology

Pitch is
tough
brave
(Focused)
determined

"Pitch began her descent, picking her way along the iron posts and prickly branches and timbs all around them."

12/18/11
P.106 They got cleo. But the animals are loose. They got nets from their boat and caught them. They are ready to put them in Savannah's shed but the boat is gone.

p.175 Max and Cass found a door they think leads to the pyramid. Prediction: They will find Benjamin along the way. I think the door behind them (the mirror one) will close and Ms. Mauvis will come. Inference: Cass is very brave, she never tooks back. Max is very smart and observant, he usally figures out riddles. Together they make a good team. They are like Max and Freak (Freak the Mighty).

The secret life of Devon Delany p.4. Devon says that she is in big trouble and she's trying to pretend she dosen't know this girl from camp. Lexi (the friend from camp) keeps calling Devon Devi but everyone else calls her Devon. I think this is really uncomfortable for Devon.

SN for 5/30/12
108 "Churcie was gone and Rosalind started to worry again" Inference: Churchie makes Rosalind feel welcome, safe, comfortable in a place where she doesn't fit in. The girls and Churchie have developed a friendship with Churchie.

110 "planned it out long ago, when Jeffrey was still a baby." Jeffery's mom and dad planned his future without him. That isn't very fair. It seems like Jeffery doesn't have much freedom.

111 "Just like Papa was

GRADE 6: *Jake, a sixth grader, who is reading a nonfiction book about Jackie Robinson, infers a character trait.*

36 "Beanballs would be thrown, I would be called names which would hurt and infuriate me, and I would be physically attacked." Jackie is being realistic because he knows that he is in for a tough time.

SYNTHESIZING

Inferring on a larger scale is called synthesizing. When we gather information from a text on a single topic and then generate an original idea based on it, we are synthesizing. For example, readers might infer a number of character traits, but when synthesizing, they will combine and use the traits to a make a statement about human nature. This is a difficult strategy to master.

Synthesizing SmartNotes Mini-Lesson for Nonfiction

(CCSS) **RI.5.8, RI.6.8, RI.7.8, RI.8.8**

> **MATERIALS**
> - Mentor text: *Night* by Elie Wiesel (teacher copy and one copy for each student)
> - Chart paper and markers or whiteboard (dry-erase or interactive) with markers
> - Student notebooks and pencils

STEP 1 **Explain the purpose of instruction.**

Think of synthesizing as making an enormous inference that can be extended to the world or human nature. When students synthesize, they take all the smaller inferences they have made and answer the following questions: *What does this mean in the world? What does this say about human beings?* When students are asked to write a thesis statement in preparation for a research project or an essay, they need to synthesize. (NB: This strategy develops the higher-order thinking required of older students. Many fifth and sixth graders are not developmentally ready for this thinking yet; however, after inferring all year, fifth and sixth graders may be ready to synthesize. Keep requiring them to make inferences, and by the time they get to eighth grade, they will be ready to synthesize.)

(Night is a complicated text. It is about a difficult topic—the Holocaust—and this first-person account is often graphic. To help students experience the text at its most powerful, we read it with few interruptions.)

Betsy: Yesterday we finished Wiesel's memoir, *Night*. It was emotionally draining—but we did a lot of good thinking, talking, and reflecting. As we prepare to start writing about our reading, we need to figure out what we want to say. After reading a book like this, there are lots of different things you might want to discuss and prove in an essay. Our work today is to figure out what some of those things might be. We are going to synthesize all our inferences, to help us say something new—something original about the world or human nature. We are going to synthesize our thinking.

STEP 2 **Demonstrate the strategy in action.**

(Our eighth graders are preparing for writing an essay. They need to synthesize what they know and say something new. They will craft a thesis statement and begin to write an essay.)

Betsy: We have spent a lot of time thinking about the world of *Night*—how it was possible that such awful things happened, and the amazing things people did to survive. One idea I would want to explore in an essay is the tenacity of the human spirit. The will to survive is stronger than we realize. This idea is never stated directly in the book. We figured this out through all the inferences we made as we read. Let's look back to our SmartNotes to see if we have evidence to support this synthesis. Let's use the ones on the board.

(Betsy pulls up the SmartNotes for *Night*, and sifts through them with students.)

Betsy: Here's a note we could use. Remember on page twenty-one when they were on the transport train to the camps, we took this SmartNote:

"We still had a few possessions left. But we never ate enough to satisfy our hunger. To save was our rule; to save up for tomorrow. Tomorrow might be worse." (p. 21) *Tomorrow—thinking about tomorrow shows that no one has given up yet—they plan on surviving.*

This Inference SmartNote, along with others we could easily find, will be used to support my synthesis that the will to survive is stronger than we know.

STEP 3 Interaction with the text.

Betsy: Work with the person next to you to sift through more of our class SmartNotes in your notebook. Look for other evidence that would support this synthesis.

(Since this thinking is complicated, Betsy gives students lots of time to work. She walks around and listens in on conversations, jumping in when needed to clarify confusion or help students stay on task.)

Betsy: Someone share a SmartNote you found that supports our idea.

Miranda: We found a SmartNote from earlier in the book when they were moved to the ghetto, before they were at the camps:

"We settled in. (What a word!) . . . Despite her own weariness, my mother began to prepare a meal. 'We must keep going, we must keep going,' she kept on repeating." (p. 18) *The mother is exhausted, she knows things are bad, but she keeps working and tries to make things good for her family.*

Betsy: That SmartNote supports our idea perfectly. Even at the beginning, when things were just starting to get bad, everyone needed to work to keep their spirits up.

(Betsy elicits more student responses, and students share their thinking.)

Betsy: Great thinking today. Tomorrow, you will get time to synthesize your own idea for an essay topic. Now, we'll move to independent reading.

(Tomorrow, students will start by rereading the class SmartNotes on *Night*, focusing on the inferences they made and synthesizing them.)

STEP 4 Practice through independent reading.

Betsy: As you read your independent reading book, think about the inferences you have been making and practice synthesizing them into your own big idea.

(Betsy has conferences while students read.)

STEP 5 Share.

(Betsy pulls the class back together after 15 minutes of independent reading.)

Donte: I'm reading *Monster* by Walter Dean Myers, and I keep making inferences about Steve and how he regrets the choices he's made.

Betsy: Donte, what is the big idea you are thinking of in regards to regret?

Donte: I'm not sure yet, but I think it's something like feeling bad and feeling regret doesn't change the bad thing you did.

Betsy: Awesome!

SYNTHESIZING SMARTNOTES SAMPLES

GRADE 5:

(top right) Lauren is reading Penny from Heaven *by Jennifer L. Holm. She makes note of the importance of freedom for children. This synthesis comes after much reading about the main character's mother.*

(bottom left) Cristina creates a list to show the new thinking she is doing about It's Raining Cupcakes *by Lisa Schroeder.*

GRADE 6:

((bottom right) Geoffrey is reading a nonfiction text about Copernicus. He once again wows us by using his background knowledge, coupled with information from the text to make new discoveries.

Title: Penny from Heaven
Author: Jennifer L. Holm

5   setting: home
Her mom seems to have a great deal of Penny's life in her control. I think it's important to let children (even 11 yr) have freedom!

86 "pop-pop, what did my father die from?" Penny asked. "What? What?" He sputters. He doesn't know. Or does he.

It's Raining Cupcakes

80 "A fire escape is really not an escape at all. Traveling to New York, now that would be an escape -IB"

   Isabel is escaping from:
1) Her mothers behavior
2) The cupcake business
3) The stress of getting money
4) All the drama

Copernicus   10/28/11

pg 84 N/A "The fourth, Bishop Dantiscus, did not get along with Copernicus. He would often challenge and antagonize him. But he still wanted Copernicus as his physician." I synthesized because earlier in the book, it said that the leader of the Teutonic Knights, his enemy, asked him to come and cure him. Here, the Bishop Dantiscus did not like him too much, but still wanted him. This is amazing, because even his enemies would want him to do it, not to lure him into a trap, but since he was the best in his ...

Using a Variety of Strategies

Sometimes, good thinking cannot be categorized into one particular strategy. Proficient readers rely on the different strategies as needed; when students are really thinking, they use a variety of reading strategies automatically. The reading strategies we have taught in mini-lessons do not exit in isolation. Students read complex texts at this age, and have to learn when to employ the different strategies. When reading a descriptive scene, for example, it makes sense for a reader to use the visualizing strategy, whereas when reading nonfiction, a reader would have to use the determining importance strategy, or else become overwhelmed by all the information. Each strategy is taught separately, but we expect that once the strategy is taught, it can be called upon because it is now part of their repertoire. SmartNotes encourage this flexibility and are evidence of the thinking that good readers engage in. The series of SmartNote samples on the next page show the range of strategies that some of our students used in their reading.

GRADE 5:

(left) Jessie is working her way through The Mysterious Benedict Society by Trenton Lee Stewart. Over three pages of text, she takes five SmartNotes, covering author's style and predictions.

(right) While reading a different book, Out of My Mind by Sharon Draper. Jessie makes a series of strong inferences. She is able to put herself in the character's situation and think like the character.

The Mysterious Benedict Society 1/14/12

p.131 "granaded and creaked like a ship at sea."
TLS uses : comparasing a lot with like areas

p.132 Mr.B wants them to read & do more, they are suprised, that there is even more to know.

p.132 after the children read all the notes, they found out that the Institute generated all its own electricity using the power of the tides.

p.133 ? "It doesn't seem that important to me. It also might have something to do with in the future a clue/or hint.
Constance got the answer

p.133 they also learned that the senders send the messages each day or for every weak signal.

Out of my mind 2/10/12

p.83 S.M.D is very descriptive when describing their daily routine.

p.85 "...rolled with laughter..."
S.M.D uses this example of personification to help the reader understand that they laughed so much together.
Difference (to show how close they are with eachother.)

p.87 Melody is thinking that she wishes she had people talk for him like Garfield does.

Inference: She is making a text-to-self connection.

With someone she enjoys listening to about and it means a lot to her that she really wishes she could talk.

GRADE 6:

(left) Samantha is reading the historical fiction novel Little Cricket by Jackie Brown. This page shows one day of her strong thinking. She lists the characters, makes connections to them, notes the setting, asks questions, and is clearly working to make sense of her reading.

(right) Emily is thinking through Flipped by Wendelin Van Draanen. She makes predictions and inferences.

(below) Giana is also reading historical fiction—The Secret School by Avi. Her thinking indicates a grasp of the time period and author's style.

Little Cricket

WIR, "Twelve-year-old Kia Vong stooped down and studied the tiny seeds nestled in the narrow dirt furrow."(1) Even though she is in Vietnam doesn't mean she's so different than me. Kia and I are almost the same age. She doesn't have the same things as me like technology, transportation, and maybe school was different too. What else could be different? Will they be forced to move away from their home because of the war in Vietnam?

WIR, "Grandfather had said Aunt Zoua was sick because one of her souls had been frightened away by the snake poison and had to be coaxed back into the body to make it whole again."(11) They believe in spirits and gods. Do they have a religion though?

Who: Kia

Flipped

pg 63 "After they cut down the sycamore tree, it seemed like everything else fell apart too." I think Juli is going through a tough time, because a lot is happening to her and her family. I think that Juli is handling everything well, because she is still doing her normal activites.

pg 114 "I wound up telling him everything." I think Chet really connects to Julianna, because he said that she reminds him of his wife. And Chet's wife died, so probably being with Juli, helps him remember his wife and makes him feel that his wife is there with him.

SmN   fiction

The Secret School   Historical
2 "The Batterd car, hicuping like a damp firecracker, swung into a sharp turn."

Here, the author uses a simile, and a metaphore.
I can really visualize the car "Hicuping" and I can really see it.

p.254 "Finn waited several more long minutes without moving, practoley without breathing."

Finn was scared, but very brave to be in there at night. ✓

When Finn hid during the film, he was a regular person, not a DHI, so he could not walk through walls and he could not push a buttin to get home.

p.258 "He could just vaguely make out willa, a good distance away, running tward him."

I have an unknown word - vaguely

I think it means bearly because if he said he could bearly make out Willa it would also make sence. ✓

Steve J.   10|28

High school   Woz pulled pranks too.

"friends" at first sight.
first "computer" blew up from scratch.
Very fast to start building.

Business

College

Illegal bluebox?
Allowed to make long distance calls for free.
he was smart, sneeky   Jobs' started
buying under priced parts at
flea markets and reselling
them to his boss at the electronics
store for a pofiti.
Still pulling pranks;
used first box to do so.
Always wanted to "push the
envelope."

TRAIT
spells words

10-5-11   Biography: Albert Einstein
pg. 52 "He simply bounce the baby
on his knee and write with the other
hand. Albert was a workaholic. It
seems very mean to just ignore
your crying baby-son and just
keep working. This is important
because he has to help his family
with work, but he also
has care for them.

pg. 67 "Put your hand on a hot stove
for a minute, and it seems like
a hour. Sit with a pretty
girl for an hour, it seems like
a minute. Thats relativity."
Albert was funny. He is comparing
a hot stove to a girl with time to help people understand.
pg. 50 "...he was overcome only by
regret that his father had died believing
him a failure." Albert was great. He
thought he failed at what he wanted
to do and he also thought his was
not proud of him. This is important
because pride from your father is very
important to a son. ✓

(top left) In a different text, Kingdom Keepers: Disney After Dark by Ridley Pearson, Giana demonstrates her knowledge of summary and uses context clues to understand unknown vocabulary.

(top right) Reading a biography of Steve Jobs, Will organizes the information he learns in a way that makes sense for him. His SmartNote format is personal: he paraphrases the text, and then makes trait inferences and inferences.

(bottom right) Gaby is reading a biography of Albert Einstein. He makes a conscious choice about the quotes he records and reflects on their importance.

Close Reading:
A Nonfiction Strategy

Close reading describes careful, text-focused reading and thinking. This strategy is most effective with nonfiction as it encourages readers to support their thinking solely with evidence from the text. Making connections and predictions will not be helpful. Readers need to be bound by the text and keep all their thinking focused on a deep understanding of it.

The Common Core State Standards place as much emphasis on reading informational text as they do on fiction, and state exams will, too. Knowing how to read nonfiction, taking close reading SmartNotes, will support readers as they manage nonfiction material and prepare for state exams.

To support our students as they read nonfiction text, we have developed a protocol, a structured conversation based on text, for them to follow. There are a series of steps to follow; at each step, questions guide students' thinking. Students read and think solely about the text in front of them. This protocol of asking questions and underlining answers to those questions can be used with the whole class, small groups, or individuals.

Close Reading Protocol

STEP 1 Preview the text.

ASK YOURSELF: What will this text be about? (Use these text features to help you answer this question.)

- Title
- Genre
- Text boxes
- Pictures
- Subtitles
- Headings
- Captions
- Organization:
  - Stanzas
  - Paragraphs
  - Bullets

UNDERLINE: Find information in the text to help you answer the question.

STEP 2 Read the first few paragraphs.

ASK YOURSELF: What is the text about at this point?

- What is happening right now?
  - Who is it about?
  - What is the problem?
  - What are you learning so far?
- Do you know when/where this takes place? Does the setting matter?
- What main ideas are developing?

UNDERLINE: Find information in the text to help you answer the questions.

STEP 3 Reading the next few paragraphs.

ASK YOURSELF: How are the people, events, and ideas developing? What are you learning?

- How is the text unfolding?
  - Is the structure chronological?
  - Is the structure cause and effect?
  - Is the structure problem and solution?
  - Is the structure question and answer?
- Is the text still about what you thought it was about?
- What is important now?
  - Add new information to the old.

UNDERLINE: Find information in the text to help you answer the questions.

STEP 4 Finish reading the text.

ASK YOURSELF: Why did the author write this text?

- What is the big idea of the text? Restate it for yourself.
- How did the text structure support the main idea?
- What is the author's purpose?
  - To inform?
  - To entertain?
  - To persuade?

UNDERLINE: Find information in the text to help you answer the questions.

The sample mini-lesson below demonstrates the use of the protocol with the whole class.

THE PROTOCOL IN ACTION

RI.5.2, RI.5.3, RI.5.8, RI.6.2, RI.6.3, RI.6.8, RI.7.2, RI.7.3, RI.7.8, RI.8.2, RI.8.3, RI.8.8

MATERIALS
- Mentor text: "Is Corn Making Us Fat?" by Sandy Fritz (a display copy and one copy for each student)
- Copy of Close Reading Protocol (page 61)
- Chart paper or whiteboard (dry-erase or interactive) and markers
- Pencils

STEP 1 Explain the purpose of instruction.

Reading nonfiction requires attention to detail. Many students are unsure of how to tackle this kind of text. They tend to either focus on unimportant information or gloss over whole swaths of information. The Close Reading Protocol is a way to teach students how to think through nonfiction texts. We guide them to stop at specific times and pose questions.

You will notice that this mini-lesson does not follow our regular format. We have eliminated the "Demonstrate the strategy in action" section because the entire protocol is done together with students—so we are modeling and practicing simultaneously.

(Betsy displays the mentor text, and distributes a copy to each student.)

Betsy: Today we will be trying a protocol—a series of steps with questions to answer, as we read a nonfiction article called "Is Corn Making Us Fat?" This protocol is going to help keep us all focused on relevant details that support the big idea.

(Betsy displays the protocol, and distributes a copy to each student.)

STEP 2 Interact with the text.

Betsy: Take a look at the protocol in front of you.

(Betsy gives students two minutes to read it.)

Betsy: What do you notice?

Steven: I noticed that we have to stop and ask ourselves questions a bunch of times.

Betsy: Good. How many times are you stopping and thinking?

Steven: Four times.

Betsy: Yes. What else do you notice?

Lina: We have to underline a lot.

Betsy: Yes, we will. Basically, we are going to read this text in chunks. Each time you stop, there will be questions to answer. You need to figure out the big ideas and find text support for them. Before we start to read, we need to do Step One, which is to preview the text. Look at the first step. What does this mean?

Rudy: We have to look at the whole thing, like how it is set up and stuff.

Betsy: Great. Yes, everyone do that. Underline features and ask yourself, What will this text be about?

(Betsy gives the students three minutes to look at features and think about what the text will be about.)

Betsy: Tony, what do you think this text will be about?

Tony: How corn is making us fat.

Betsy: Which features help you think that?

Tony: I see fact, myth, opinion circles, and a quote that says fast food has corn.

Betsy: Other people, what do you think this text will be about?

Sarah: I see subheadings: "Think Fresh." Maybe this is about eating healthy?

Todd: I think Sarah may be right, I see a list of ways to eat smart.

Betsy: What else?

Todd: Oh, there was a funny picture—a cartoon about a Mom trying to pack a healthy lunch.

Betsy: So far, there seem to be two main ideas—corn makes us fat and ways to eat healthy. As we read on, your job is to find text details that support one or both of these claims/main ideas. Before I ask you to read on, underline with your pencil the features we discussed. I will do the same on the board.

(Betsy gives students two minutes to do this.)

Betsy: Now we are ready to move onto Step Two of the protocol. Read the first two paragraphs and ask yourself what the text is starting to be about. You need to focus on who it is about, what the problem is, and what you are learning so far. When you find information that helps you think about the ideas that are developing, underline them with your pencil.

(Betsy gives students four minutes to read, think, and underline.)

Betsy: Say something.

Finn: I found proof of what Tony said. Corn is making us fat.

Betsy: What did you underline?

Finn: I underlined this: "More than a quarter of [items in a supermarket] contain corn."

Betsy: Everyone, be sure to underline that fact. I will do it on the board, too. Did anyone find information to support our second claim that it is important to eat healthy?

(Students shake their heads.)

Betsy: When I was walking around before, I didn't notice anyone underline any words in boldface. Let's look at those together. It says, **"The number of overweight kids in the US has tripled since 1980. Meanwhile, the amount of corn being added to our foods has risen dramatically. Is there a connection?"** What is the author trying to tell us here?

Tony: Yeah, corn is making us fat.

Betsy: Yes, the author is saying there is a connection between corn in foods and overweight kids. Let's underline that quote. Now we are ready to move to Step Three. Read the next few paragraphs, stopping at "Think Fresh," and think about what is important now—and how the ideas are developing. In other words, add more information to the claims/big ideas we are supporting. Underline the new information.

(Betsy gives students five minutes to read, think, and underline.)

Betsy: This is complicated. What new information did you learn?

Trevor: Corn has lots of calories and sugar. And, it is cheap. And they feed it to cows—which we eat.

Betsy: So . . . someone put this together.

Trevor: I got this: We eat the cows that ate the corn—the corn has all those calories so we get the calories, so we get fat.

Betsy: Does that make sense, everybody? There is a cause-and-effect relationship between what we feed animals and what happens to the person who eats it. The author helps us see that connection through those great subheadings and that prominent quote. (Class nods.) What other information did you lean?

Beatrice: Scientists invented HFCS to make things sweet. It comes from corn, and it is cheap.

Betsy: How does this fit with our claim that corn makes us fat?

Beatrice: They said that corn syrup sweetens a lot of stuff and so like Trevor said, we eat that stuff—so we get fat.

Betsy: Nice job. Everyone underline the details that support this thinking. I'll underline it as well.

(Betsy gives the students a minute to do this.)

Betsy: Before we move on and finish the text, remember that there is another claim: there are ways for people to eat healthy. If we don't find more evidence to support this, we might have to eliminate it.

Step Four requires that you read to the end of the article, and ask yourself why the author wrote this text and what the central idea is. When you find information to support your thinking, don't forget to underline it.

(Betsy gives the students eight minutes to read, think, and underline.)

Betsy: Okay, let's wrap this up. Why did the author write this text? What is she trying to tell readers?

Perri: The author, Sandy Fritz, wants us to know that corn is making us fat and we should eat healthy.

Betsy: Support that with the text.

Perri: That whole last paragraph and the list on the side is about ways to eat healthy because, like she said, we are eating too much corn and HFCS.

Betsy: Okay, there were two claims, both were supported. Which do you think is the central idea or claim?

Dora: Corn makes us fat, but remember to eat healthy.

Betsy: What is the author's purpose?

Dora: To tell us this information.

Betsy: Yes, her purpose is to inform us. Good hard work, everyone. At lunch today, remember this text.

Close reading is a skill that all readers need. As you noticed, readers are not going beyond the text—instead they are required to dig deeper, focusing on the text itself. This results in a full analysis of the text by students: how it was presented and what they learned.

After teaching the protocol to your whole class a few times, use it in small groups to encourage everyone to participate and target thinking. Once internalized, these questions support readers when reading independently and in all genres.

Conclusion

Mini-lesson topics come from the reading strategies students need to be successful readers. Modeling SmartNotes through the shared-class text is a robust mode of teaching a strategy and practicing it. Showing his or her thinking through SmartNotes and being able to move fluidly from one strategy to another are signs of a proficient reader. Whether reading fiction or nonfiction, student thinking must be tied to the text. The SmartNote structure encourages students to be true to the text as they deepen their thinking.

CHAPTER FOUR

Assessing Students' Thinking Through SmartNotes

SmartNotes are not only a way to hold students accountable for their reading, but they also provide valuable assessment data.

- We periodically read students' SmartNote notebooks to evaluate their thinking at a particular point in time and also over time. This is our data source for students' grades.

- In conferences, SmartNotes allow us to assess a student's thinking, and we use them as a formative assessment. What the formative assessment reveals helps us plan our instruction for the next day.

- After students learn the structure of a SmartNote (text evidence and their thinking), they are ready to be pushed. Requiring them to add a "So What?" to their SmartNotes thinking portion ensures that they are doing more than mindlessly spitting text back to us; it proves that their thinking is deep and thoughtful. It is not enough for students just to notice reading strategies, they must also notice and write about why using the strategies matters. They must answer the question, "So what?"

A Quick Snapshot of Student Thinking

When we want immediate data on how effectively students comprehend their reading, we ask students to complete a SmartNotes Check Sheet for a text. As you can see, it contains all the elements of a SmartNote for a text on one page. A reproducible appears on page 112.

This glimpse into students' thinking is quick, effective, and easy to grade using a SmartNotes Rubric. A reproducible appears on page 113.

SAMPLE SMARTNOTES CHECK SHEETS

The following sample SmartNotes Check Sheets and rubrics all come from fifth graders.

Lauren's work displays her unique SmartNote-taking strategy. For each quote she records, she first summarizes the information and then adds an inference. See how we graded her on the rubric.

Jessica's work, another example of strong thinking, shows the variety of strategies she uses in her thinking. Again, see how we graded her on the rubric.

Max uses his SmartNotes Check Sheet to keep track of character traits and connections by writing a SmartNote about a different character.

The group of student SmartNotes Check Sheets at the right contain more teacher writing as these students needed to be pushed to do more or deeper thinking.

In these samples, it is harder to see the connection between the quote and the student's thinking.

While Harris (left) and Olivia (right) have made good decisions where to stop and think in their texts, they need to be pushed to think more deeply.

The examples at the right show more gaps in these students' thinking. The thinking displayed is not particularly thoughtful and reflects some confusion or lack of understanding.

Tracking Students' Thinking Over Time

The power of these SmartNotes Check Sheets is that they also give you the ability to track students' thinking over time. We do SmartNote checks often, as they are quick and easy assessments. In these days of CCSS and teacher accountability, SmartNote checks are evidence of student growth, and can be direct evidence of teaching.

SAMPLE SMARTNOTES CHECK SHEETS

In December, our comments on Ally's SmartNotes Check Sheet reflected the need for her to explain more of her thinking. She was pushed to try different strategies and, in particular, to make inferences. By May, her SmartNotes Check Sheet showed greater facility with inferences, asking smart questions, and including a lot of her own thinking. Her spring SmartNotes almost appear to be from a different student! Wow!

The SmartNotes Check Sheets on the next page focus on nonfiction. These fifth graders were given two short texts, "About Gary Paulsen" and "About the Iditarod." Their SmartNotes don't contain page numbers because both texts were short magazine articles. Again, SmartNote checks are a great tool for us to see if students understand a text.

Ally: December

Ally: May

Independent Reading in the Age of Common Core © 2013 by Sue Cannone-Calick & Elizabeth Henley • Scholastic Teaching Resources

Daniela

Isha

Daniela does a good job of picking good stopping places and choosing pertinent quotes to think about. Her thinking reflects a solid understanding of the text. Her thinking includes questions and reflections, proving to us that Daniela was "present" while reading.

Isha's thinking is another good example of solid thinking through nonfiction. You will notice a variety of thinking strategies that, again, indicate truly active reading.

Emma does some great thinking around the article on Gary Paulsen. In particular, she uses what she learned (details) to ask a big question. The ability to ask a good question cannot be understated. Using what she learned about Paulsen's many jobs, Emma wonders about his life path.

Ruthie is also able to think about the big ideas in "About Gary Paulsen." Her final SmartNote, in fact, hints at the author's message/purpose.

Emma

Ruthie

Using SmartNotes in a Conference

Conferring is an invaluable component of the balanced-literacy model. Talking to individual students during independent reading time (near the end of each mini-lesson) about their reading and their thinking is what conferring is all about. Conferences are a valuable one-on-one instructional practice that enables on-the-spot assessment and instruction.

During a conference, the teacher and student sit together to talk about the student's reading. You can pull up a chair right next to the student, meet at your desk, or sit at a table— wherever you are both comfortable. Through this dialogue, you can find a strength or weakness for the student to focus on and then ask pointed questions to get to your teaching point. All students are reading independently as we have conferences. Over the course of a week, it is our goal to have a conference with each student.

A student's SmartNotes are the perfect way to launch a conference. Information about the books that students are reading, the strategies they are using, and their thoughts about the texts are recorded in their SmartNote notebooks, so even if you're not familiar with the book a student is reading, you can still engage in a beneficial conversation.

ASKING QUESTIONS

All our conferences begin with the same question: "Would you please show me your SmartNotes?" Then, after reading what the student has written, we move on to questions and prompts, such as the following:

- "Why did you write this?"
- "Why do you think this is important?"
- "What did you think when you read that?"
- "Explain this idea."
- "How did you figure this out?"
- "What do you mean here?"
- "What strategy did you use here?"
- "Say more about this."

Between what you see on a SmartNote and what students say in response to your follow-up questions, you will be able to get an accurate picture of your readers.

Your job during a conference is to record the conversation. Write down the questions you ask and the student's responses. A written history of the conversation is transcribed in the student's notebook, right next to the SmartNote. This record can be referenced by you or the student. This data is beneficial on many levels: students can and should look back at our notes to them; we can refer back to them to remember previous conversations; parents can glean how their child is performing by reading these notes; and last, this data can be used for teacher evaluation.

DIRECT INSTRUCTION

The purpose of a one-on-one conference is to provide direct instruction to a student. A main tenet of this process is that after talking, the teacher leaves the student with a task—something he or she can then practice independently until the next conference. Here is a sampling of tasks:

- "Write down the exact words from the text to support your thought."
- "Try answering your questions."
- "Check your predictions."
- "Try a different reading strategy."
- "Collect more evidence to support that character trait."
- "Don't forget to add your thinking to your strategy thinking."
- "Keep reading and thinking—you're doing great."
- "Don't forget to add how that connection will help you understand the text better."

CONFERENCE OBSERVATIONS THROUGH THE YEAR

In the beginning of the year, you may notice that the reader—

- knows what is happening in the book.
- is able to summarize.
- makes connections.
- understands character traits.
- is able to make inferences.
- uses a variety of reading strategies.
- is asking thoughtful questions.

Later in the year, you may notice that the reader—

- recognizes beautiful language.
- notices an author's style.
- is able to determine theme.
- is able to connect themes/ideas/characters in multiple texts.

Independent Reading in the Age of Common Core © 2013 by Sue Cannone-Calick & Elizabeth Henley • Scholastic Teaching Resources

- "Reread when you get confused again."
- "Write down those new words and try to guess what they mean."
- "Synthesize. What is your new thinking?"
- "Add your So What?"

So often, teachers wonder if students remember their good advice and follow through on the mini-lesson instruction they give. To ensure our students don't forget what we've discussed—we leave our notes right in the notebook, ending with the task we want kids to complete before our next conference.

USING SMARTNOTES AS A FORMATIVE ASSESSMENT

In addition to being an archive of student work, the SmartNotes in a student's notebook generate good formative assessment data and can influence your whole-class instruction. A formative assessment can be any task you assign in which you use the student product to inform your instruction. In other words, this type of assessment is a quick snapshot of how your students are performing at a certain point in time. A formative assessment based on a student's SmartNotes is an organic assessment and produces great data. SmartNotes can be used to show a student's growth, signal the need for additional support, and/or inform parents during conferences. Additionally, the notebook full of SmartNotes provides solid evidence of student achievement and growth toward state and local goals.

SAMPLE CONFERENCES: FICTION

This section contains transcripts of conferences with students who are reading a variety of genres.

Alex is reading the first book in the NERDS series by Michael Buckley, NERDS: National Espionage, Rescue, and Defense Society. *He often has trouble finding a just-right text and tends to abandon texts quickly. Alex has started a new book, and Sue wants to make sure it is a good fit and that he's on the right track.*

Sue: Would you please show me your SmartNotes from *NERDS*?

(She reads what Alex has written: *Jackson was telling his dad about the NERD club and that's why he missed class. The principal said he would get suspended for three days. His dad punished Jackson by taking away all electronics until his grades go up.*)

Sue: You wrote a summary. Let me see if I understand what you mean: Jackson is suspended for three days, so he can't go to school and will miss NERD meetings. Am I right?

Alex: Yes.

Sue: Why do you think this is important?

Alex: Jackson is upset. His dad doesn't believe him about the NERDS.

Sue: That's interesting. How did Jackson get involved with the NERDS?

Alex: I feel bad for him because it wasn't his idea—he was forced, and now he is part of this group.

Sue: With everything you know about Jackson, how do you think he will handle this problem? Make a prediction.

Alex: I think he will try to figure out a way to go.

Sue: Do mean he will figure out a way to escape from the house and go to the meeting?

Alex: Yes.

Sue: Good prediction. Now here is your task: I will write it right here: *See if your prediction is true. How does Jackson manage to get back to the NERDS? Be sure to use the direct words from the text to support your thinking.*

Debrief: Although Sue was not familiar with this book, she was still able to figure out that Alex was understanding the plot because his summary was clear, and he was using reading strategies appropriately—he was able to make a reasonable prediction. Encouraging Alex to monitor his predictions will keep him invested in figuring things out and on track with the plot. Sue was left with important information about her student. A day or two later, when Sue is able to check in on Alex again, a quick read of his SmartNotes will indicate if he is still on track or if further instruction is needed.

Sam is also reading a book in a series, Diary of a Wimpy Kid, Book One *by Jeff Kinney. Betsy knows that Sam is a reluctant reader. He is often distracted, and struggles to think deeply through a text and to record that thinking.*

Betsy: Would you please show me your SmartNotes?

Sam: I am having trouble with them.

Betsy: Say more about that.

Sam: I don't know what to write.

Betsy: Let's read together. When you get to the bottom of the page, we'll talk about what each of us is thinking.

(Betsy and Sam read page 2 of the book.)

Betsy: Okay, what did you think was important?

Sam: Greg says he is in the middle of morons.

Betsy: Let's write down what Jeff Kinney actually wrote: "I am stuck in the middle of a bunch of morons." (p. 2) What did you think when you read that?

Sam: I do not think Greg is going to have a good year.

Betsy: Smart. Let's write that down too: *I do not think Greg is going to have a good year.*

What does that mean? Make an inference.

Sam: He is negative. He is a complainer.

Betsy: Let's write that down too: *He is negative. He is a complainer.*

Betsy: You found a good character trait. Why is Greg's being negative important? What's the big idea?

Sam: The big idea is that not getting along well is going to be a problem for Greg.

Betsy: Let's add that to your SmartNotes: *Not getting along well is going to be a problem for Greg.* Here is your task: *Try to make Inference SmartNotes as you read; they will help you get to the big idea like you just did.*

Debrief: Betsy's strategy of reading the text along with Sam was a good one because Sam knew she would help him identify his thinking. Sam struggles to think deeply. Go back and notice the questions Betsy asked. The questions were short, clear, and directed to push Sam to get to the big idea. They scaffolded his thinking. Later, when Betsy checks in on Sam again, she will be able to see evidence of his thinking in his SmartNotes.

Samples of SmartNotes and conference notes are shown at the right. Teacher writing is visible and in some cases brief.

Noelle's Sample: This is a good example of the power of a conference to push a reader to the next level. Through questioning the thinking Noelle had already done, Sue was able to leave her with the task to think more deeply and record the So What?

Nick's Sample: In this conference, Sue records a paraphrased version of their conversation summarizing the text. Often, the conversations are too long or detailed to record word for word. Later, she leaves Nick with the following task: *Push yourself and use more strategies as you read.*

SAMPLE CONFERENCES: NONFICTION

In a conference, the discussion is the same for fiction and nonfiction. The goal is to find out what students are already thinking and to push them further, or to clarify confusion and set them straight.

Michael is reading Chasing Lincoln's Killer *by James L. Swanson.*

Sue: Hey, Michael, would you please show me your SmartNotes?

Michael: Right now, I just read the part when Lewis Powell went to Seward's house.

Sue: Show me your thinking in your SmartNotes.

Michael: I made a picture in my head about this: "Before him stood a tall, attractive, muscular man, well dressed in fine leather boots, black pants, jacket, and hat. He was holding a small package in his hands. The deception had worked." (p. 49)

Noelle is reading Jeremy Fink and the Meaning of Life *by Wendy Mass. Noelle is a proficient sixth-grade reader who clearly shows her thinking in her SmartNotes.*

Nick is reading Miss Peregrine's Home for Peculiar Children *by Ransom Riggs.*

Sue: Tell me why this is important.

Michael: It's cool. I saw Powell trying to get in to assassinate Seward.

Sue: All that from this quote?

Michael: No, look here: "Powell and the servant argue for about five minutes. Powell desperately wants to get upstairs to where Seward is so he can kill him and looking normal will help him."

Sue: Okay, that makes more sense. Your visualizing is helping you not only see the people, but the action too. Let's each look at the photos on page fifty and read page fifty-one and then talk about what else we can visualize to understand Powell and what he is doing.

(Sue and Michael read page 51 to themselves and look at the black-and-white photos and captions on page 50.)

Sue: You are right, Michael, this is exciting. What did you visualize?

Michael: I saw Powell determined to get upstairs to complete his mission.

Sue: Let's talk more about that. Be more specific. What do you see Powell doing?

Michael: I see him holding onto that little box and using it to get upstairs.

Sue: You're right. That box is really important. We're going to write a SmartNote now. Go back to the text and find a quote to show the importance of the box.

Michael: This one. I'll write it in my notebook: "Incredibly, Powell, thanks to the little package he showed as a prop, had still not created suspicion about his true intentions." (p. 51)

Sue: Add your thinking now.

Michael: I see Powell holding onto this box, and I see his determination.

Sue: Excellent way to use visualizing to understand a character.

Debrief: In this conference, it was clear that Michael was enjoying and understanding this complex and interesting nonfiction text. His interest made it possible to push him to use the text effectively. Having a clear picture of what was going on allowed Michael to do higher order thinking—make inferences about the characters. Sue's questioning, and insistence upon textual evidence, helped Michael practice close reading, and use the text details to support his good ideas.

Using SmartNotes to Plan for Instruction

Data culled from conferences is helpful not only at that moment; we use data from our students' SmartNotes to plan future instruction. The data indicates the strengths and weaknesses of individual students and the class as a whole: SmartNotes inform us about individual, small-group, and whole-class needs.

CONFERENCE RECORD KEEPING

Keeping records of conferences is crucial for planning future instruction. In addition to individual notes kept in students' notebooks, we maintain a Weekly Conference Log (see page 114). The log creates a visual record of what we taught each student. After each conference, we jot the task we assigned to the reader in the log. At the end of each week, the completed log creates a clear picture of what instruction students need. Issues that show up a lot are ideal mini-lesson topics; other problems that appear only a few times will require either additional one-on-one conferences or small-group instruction. Additionally, having all our teaching points recorded in one place simplifies the start of follow-up conferences. Sue may say to Sam, for example: "The other day Ms. Henley told you to keep taking inference notes to help you with figuring out the big idea. Let's see your new SmartNotes." Holding conferences on a regular basis and being steadfast in record keeping is the only way to truly know your readers.

At the right is a sample of a Weekly Conference Log for the week of February 6–10. As you can see, we fill it in with information from our conferences.

Debrief: At the end of the week, we studied the patterns that developed. Laying out our data, we noticed the following:

- One student needed work to stop reading ahead. We would address this in another one-to-one conference.

- One student needed to work on adding his or her thinking to the quote. This, too, would be worked on in a one-on-one conference.

- Two students needed to work on using what they know about a series to help them delve deeper into their understanding. This would be addressed in a one-on-two conference or a very small group.

- Two students needed guidance with finding a just-right book. This will also be addressed in a one-on-two conference.

- Two students needed to work on broadening the strategies they use. We would also handle this is in a one-on-two conference.

- Two students needed help finding evidence to support their thinking. This would be a one-on-two conference.

- Three students needed help finding good places to stop and think. This is an ideal teaching point for small-group instruction.

- Seven students will need help adding the So What? to their SmartNotes. Because this represents a large portion of the class, it makes sense to address it with the whole class. This mini-lesson will be repeated a few times throughout the remainder of the year, so it's okay that not all students have mastered it.

Our instruction varies week to week, depending on the needs of our class. Again, using SmartNotes and conference data informs us by providing an up-to-the-minute account of students' strengths and weaknesses.

SMALL-GROUP WORK

Every week, based on the data in our Weekly Conference Log, we pull at least one small group of students who need to work on a particular strategy or who have a similar need.

The two small-group instruction samples below are based on a week in which we noticed that many of our conferences focused on character traits. One group needed support in thinking between the lines—actually making an inference about a character trait. Students in this group were somewhat literal thinkers. The other group was able to make these inferences, but their SmartNotes lacked text support. These two groups had similar needs, yet none of the students in either group would be supported by instruction in a whole-class setting.

SMALL GROUP: MAKING INFERENCES ABOUT A CHARACTER TRAIT

Betsy: Open your notebooks to the class SmartNotes we made yesterday about the characters in *The Outsiders*. Yesterday, when we were reading, we talked about how we learned about Ponyboy through his actions. Ponyboy talked with Cherry after he rescued her from Dally at the movie theater; they talked about sunsets.

Elizabeth: That was cool because Ponyboy wants so bad to be tough.

Betsy: Say more about that.

James: His brothers and friends are all cool dudes—the Greasers are all supposed to be tough.

Betsy: Let's get back to what we saw Ponyboy do. What trait would describe his behavior?

Eric: He was nice to a girl.

Betsy: Yes, we even have a vocabulary word this week that would fit perfectly with what you just said, Eric.

James: *Gallant.*

Hannah: Oh, yeah. *Gallant* fits—he is being gentlemanly.

Betsy: When you are reading your independent book, you need to do the same kind of thinking we just did. Read those books now and look for traits to describe a character. Look back at the last few SmartNotes you took—you may get some ideas that way.

(Students read and take SmartNotes for about 12 minutes as Betsy has whispered conversations. Betsy rotates through this group of independent readers. She leans over their shoulders to see what they are writing/thinking. If needed, she will prompt and/or have a quick, quiet chat.)

Betsy: Okay, let's hear some of the traits you found—and how.

Hannah: I'm reading *Flipped*. Julianna is smart.

Betsy: How do you know?

Hannah: She figured out how to make an incubator and hatch eggs at home.

Betsy: Does that make sense to the rest of you?

(Students nod and mumble yes.)

Betsy: Now, when you go back to your seats, keep reading and taking SmartNotes and making character trait inferences. Thank you, everyone.

 Independent Reading in the Age of Common Core © 2013 by Sue Cannone-Calick & Elizabeth Henley • Scholastic Teaching Resources

Debrief: We find that by referring back to the class text when we pull a small group, students have a common focus. Yes, it can be unnerving to have a group reading different texts, but the focus is the strategy—not the plot—so it really doesn't matter. Even though students were not all reading the same book, Betsy was able to support their thinking through the class text. The intensity level in a small group is high, as all students need to participate. These literal-minded students now know to look at character behavior to help them make inferences. Later in the year, groups might focus on using dialogue or what other characters think or say to help with characterization. Students know that in the small-group setting they must attempt the strategy work. The close scrutiny we do does not allow students to fake it or opt out of participating.

SMALL GROUP: TEXT SUPPORT FOR CHARACTER TRAIT INFERENCES

Sue: Open up your SmartNotes to a character trait you found yesterday when you were reading your independent book. Let's share some.

Charlotte: I'm reading *When Zachary Beaver Came to Town*, and I think Toby is inconsiderate.

Sue: How do you know? And I want you all to hear the way Charlotte thinks this through.

Charlotte: Well, Toby's best friend's brother died, and he didn't want to go to the funeral. It was too hard for him—he never thought about how hard it is for Cal.

Sue: Okay—inconsiderate is a great trait for you to find here—and you proved it well. Does it count if a character is only inconsiderate once?

David: No. You said before—it only is a trait if the person is like that a lot.

Sue: Good listening. So, Charlotte, do you still say that Toby is inconsiderate?

Charlotte: Yes, and I'll tell you why. He is snotty to his dad, won't read the letters his mom wrote him and, again, didn't go to Cal's brother's funeral.

Sue: Great thinking, Charl. You guys were all able to infer a character trait—but it is not enough. You need evidence from the text.

David: She just told you.

Sue: Yes, but a strong SmartNote has both the inference and the evidence from the text. Your job now is to go back to the SmartNote you took yesterday to find the character trait you identified, and go back through the text to find the proof to support it.

(Sue gives students about ten minutes to search their notebooks and independent reading books.)

Charlotte: I think I found it. I am writing it down now: ". . . but I drag out my bike from the garage and hop on. And instead of turning right, toward the church, I think left, lean into the wind and ride. . . . My bike and I become one, and we don't stop until we are in front of the Bowl-A-Rama." (p. 168)

Sue: Excellent. You found text support that Toby didn't attend the funeral, supporting your inference that he is inconsiderate. Once you all find your quote to support your inference, you can go back to your desks and keep taking SmartNotes.

Debrief: Notice that Sue did not refer to the class text in this group. It wasn't necessary. The focus of this group was on finding evidence in a text. Don't be wary of trying this; it is really okay that students come to the group with different books. The thinking is the same, even though the plot and characters are different.

This group was able to make character trait inferences and to explain their thinking. All that was missing was text evidence; text support is an important element of a SmartNote. Text support validates students' thinking. With it, they have proof. They have evidence that says "Here's how I know this." This is powerful. This is the kind of thinking we want from our students. And when we see students' thinking in their SmartNotes notebook, we have yet more data showing what they truly understand.

Introducing So What? Thinking: Building "Reading Swag"

There is so much going on at the mid-point of the year. Your readers are good thinkers now, and their SmartNotes prove it. You have been teaching mini-lessons, conferring with your readers, paying attention to their levels of comprehension, and reading and reading and reading! Students should be lauded and applauded for their SmartNote thinking. This "reading swag," —students' reading confidence—is obvious and should be celebrated. Your students are proud, and they should be! At this point of the year, you may observe that taking SmartNotes comes easily to students, but their notes may sound rote and repetitive. When you read them, you are left wondering, "So what?" By then, students understand the reading strategies; their independent reading stamina is increasing; they are reflecting on their thinking and recording their thoughts. Borrowing from Norton Juster's *The Phantom Tollbooth*, students enter the doldrums when they don't think. The doldrums are a place where students' work seems dull and boring and lacks enthusiasm and effort. Alas, sometimes students' SmartNotes get stuck in the doldrums. Look at this SmartNote from *When Zachary Beaver Came to Town* by Kimberly Willis Holt:

> "And instead of turning right towards the church, I turn left, lean into the wind, and ride. I jump sidewalk curbs and skim corners on the turns. My bike and I become one, and we don't stop until we are in front of the Bowl-a-Rama." (p. 168). *I can infer that Toby is upset about Wayne's death and that is why he is avoiding going to the church.*

Yes, the SmartNote shows that this student made an inference about the character, and yes, the reader has a good handle on this part of the text, but the SmartNote needs to show deeper thinking. On the surface, this is fine; this, in fact, is what we have been asking students to record, but there is more thinking to be done here. The SmartNote is flat and mechanical; it truly doesn't show real deep thinking: this is what we mean by a rote SmartNote. After reading this SmartNote, we are left wishing the reader had connected this inference to bigger thinking about the text: *Why does it matter that Toby is upset? What does this reveal about Toby? How does this affect the plot? Why is this moment significant?* In other words, once students have a handle on strategies, just using them is no longer enough; their active thinking must be evident.

Later, when we asked these questions (what we call "So What?" questions), the reader added the following reflections:

Toby doesn't know how to deal with his sadness. It matters because Toby is selfish. He is hurting and can't see that so is Cal. Missing the funeral is a bad idea. Cal needs him to be a friend right now.

This further reflection shows that the reader was able to identify the big idea of friendship in the text.

METACOGNITION

Having students think about their own thinking (i.e., engaging in metacognition) is a good way to get them out of the doldrums. At the mid-point of your year, it is valuable to have students stop and reflect on their SmartNote taking. Pose the following question: *How has taking SmartNotes helped you be a better reader?* Use the information in the box at the right to deepen students' thinking about this question.

The samples below show students' work when Sue asked her sixth graders to reassess their SmartNotes.

Samantha: Samantha notices her need to clarify confusion. Noticing this about herself is important for her to become a better reader. She recognizes that Question SmartNotes support her understanding and allow her to "organize her thoughts" and enjoy the reading.

Heenal: Heenal goes back to a previously taken SmartNote and adds new thinking to an inference. She realizes her original inference is incomplete. Rereading SmartNotes is powerful. Good for her! (The SmartNote on the next page shows Heenal's decision to abandon a book.)

START AT THE BEGINNING OF YOUR SMARTNOTE NOTEBOOK AND LOOK THROUGH YOUR SMARTNOTES.

- What do you notice about the kinds of SmartNotes you have taken?

- Organize and categorize your SmartNotes.

- Think about your thinking. Be honest. If you really haven't been thinking through the books you read, note that.

- Write down your observations on the next clean page of your notebook:

- I take _____ .

- My SmartNotes _____ .

- I noticed _____ .

- Did my fall SmartNotes record more in-depth thinking? Why?

- I want to try _____ .

- I want to get back to _____ .

Now, go back to an old SmartNote and try to expand it.

- I used to think _____ , but now I think _____ .

- Add new thinking to a SmartNote. Freewrite off of your note. See where your thinking takes you!

- Upon further thinking, I _____ .

Samantha

Heenal

> I don't very much like, "The Graveyard Book" By Neil Gaiman because it sometimes gets very confusing. At one time Bod, the main character, would be learning letters and at another time though there would suddenly be ghosts talking to him. I do though like mysteries, but this one is not like others I have read. In the beginning, although it caught my attention with the murderer killing different people in the house, after that, nothing that exciting occured. That is why I chose to abandon the book.

Heenal

> Smartnote thinking
>
> When I take my smartnotes I noticed that it all depends on the book because when I read the Secret series I noticed. that most of my smartnotes were questions because the whole book is about a mystery so as a reader you have questions about what you read. As a reader that can also help you to figure out what the secret is. In the Mother Daughter Book Club series the writing style is much different so my smartnotes were very different, most of my smartnotes were about word choice and figurative language. The authors of these 2 books were very different because the Secret series author just wanted to get the point across but the Mother Daughter Book Club series author went into greater detail about everything. i

Sophia

Sophia: Sophia recognized that she needs to take different types of SmartNotes depending on the genre of the text she is reading. Her about-the-text thinking demonstrates an understanding of author's purpose and how it affects readers. Wow! As a sixth grader, Sophia is clearly a sophisticated thinker and, as a result, a thoughtful reader. We were blown away by her metacognition.

This kind of metacognitive thinking shows that readers 1) know how their thinking has grown and 2) can reflect on the strategy of taking SmartNotes and how it has supported them. SmartNotes are a good gauge of thinking—and promote the metacognitive thinking required to be a better reader. Middle schoolers are capable of this thinking through vigorous SmartNote taking. Metacognition is a difficult thought process, requiring modeling and practice. A sample mini-lesson to help develop students' metacognition appears below.

MINI-LESSON

Threads of Thinking (Metacognition) SmartNotes Mini-Lesson

MATERIALS
- Chart paper or whiteboard (dry-erase or interactive) and markers
- Student notebooks and pens or pencils

STEP 1 Explain the purpose of instruction.

At the mid-point of the school year, asking readers to look back at all the thinking they have done so far is a good way to get them to feel a sense of pride over their hard work and, more important, to notice the kinds of thinking they have done. This reflection is ultimately intended to push readers into thinking more deeply.

(To use their SmartNotes to delve more deeply into a text, students need to look back and evaluate their past SmartNotes.)

Betsy: We have read many books so far this year, and our SmartNotes demonstrate the good thinking we have done. Today we are going to ask you to spend some time rereading your SmartNotes. Rereading your SmartNotes is a good thing to do. Why do you think we would want you to do this?

(Students share answers such as "To remember what we read?" or "To see what we thought about at the beginning of the year?")

Betsy: Smart thinking. We want you to reread your SmartNotes for all those reasons. We also want you to notice all the different kinds of thinking you have tried and notice some things about yourself as a reader.

STEP 2 Demonstrate the strategy in action.

(Betsy displays her own SmartNote on the interactive whiteboard.)

Betsy: Here are three pages of my own SmartNotes from *The Scorpio Races* by Maggie Stiefvater. In rereading them, I notice many SmartNotes about setting. This book takes place on an island where the sea plays an important role. I have noticed that I keep thinking of the sea. It's a thread I keep thinking about. The sea is important to understanding Puck, the main character, and the choices she makes. I also have SmartNotes about great words I fell in love with and phrases I thought were really cool.

STEP 3 Interact with the text.

(Betsy pulls up pages from the class *Hatchet* SmartNotes, and the conversation continues.)

Betsy: Let's go back to the first days of *Hatchet* and look together at those class SmartNotes. I will read our notes aloud, while you follow along in your notebook. Turn to your first page of *Hatchet* SmartNotes.

(Betsy reads aloud from the class SmartNotes, while students follow the version in their notebooks.)

Betsy: What do you notice about our SmartNotes?

(Students respond, noticing that many SmartNotes are about Brian.)

Betsy: Good observations. Let's jot that thread down in the margin.

(Betsy writes in the margin "Brian Observations," and students do the same in their notebooks.)

Betsy: Let's read on and see if we can find other threads. What else do you notice?

(Betsy gives students time to reread and think. They notice that we took notes on how Paulsen writes many one-word sentences and paragraphs.)

Betsy: Well done! We did notice aspects of Gary Paulsen's writing style. Let's add that thread to the margin of our SmartNotes.

(Betsy and the students write, "Gary Paulsen's writing style" in the margin of the SmartNotes.)

Betsy: When you start work in a few minutes, continue to do this: First, reread your SmartNotes from one of the books you read this year, and ask yourself, "What did I take SmartNotes about?" "What did I notice?" Then, write your observations in the margin. Notice what your threads are. Remember that I noticed a thread about setting and word choice, and we noticed threads about character and author's style. At the end of work time today, we will ask some of you to share your thinking.

STEP 4 Practice through independent work.

Students return to their work, with notebooks open, sifting through their SmartNotes. We confer with students about what they notice.

STEP 5 Share.

Betsy: We noticed some great thinking today. Sam, what threads did you notice in your thinking?

Sam: In my last book, *Rodrick Rules,* I thought a lot about character.

Betsy: That's great. Olivia, why don't you tell us what you noticed?

(Olivia responds and we get one or two others to share.)

Betsy: You all did a great job today. When we pick up with this tomorrow, we will see how these threads help us figure out the kinds of readers we are and push us to deeper thinking.

From this point forward, things can go in a number of directions. Sometimes, students notice intriguing patterns of thought and show interest in exploring them. More often, however, after sifting, we notice that students are limiting themselves to only certain strategies or repeating favorite ones. Yet another, and perhaps more typical, outcome is that students don't notice any significant patterns in their thinking. This scenario may cause you and your students some discomfort, but don't worry. Conferences and more conversation will eventually lead them to find a pattern. It's okay if you provide the thread for struggling students. Once students have found a thread (or been given one), supporting that thread through text evidence is the next step. Following and supporting that thread is students' work.

After the initial conversation around finding threads, it is time for the crucial work of using and developing these ideas.

Say Something SmartNote Mini-Lesson

MINI-LESSON

> **MATERIALS**
> • Chart paper or whiteboard (dry-erase or interactive) and markers
> • Student notebooks and pens or pencils

STEP 1 Explain the purpose of instruction.

Students have recognized and noted the threads of their thinking. The purpose of this lesson is to help them see that these threads can be developed and used in many different ways.

(Sue pulls up the *Hatchet* class SmartNotes with observations in the margins.)

Sue: Let's review the thread work we did the other day. We noticed that a lot of our *Hatchet* SmartNotes were about Brian, and many were also about Gary Paulsen's writing style. Those threads are written right here in the margin. You also noticed threads from your own SmartNotes. Noticing our smart thinking is great, but there is more to it. Once you notice a thread, something you have been focusing on, your job is to develop that idea/thread and add to it: say something about it.

STEP 2 Demonstrate the strategy in action.

Sue: What is an idea/thread we have been formulating about Brian?

(Sue gives students time to reread a few class SmartNotes and think.)

Michael: He is brave.

Sue: Yes, we have many SmartNotes about Brian's bravery.

Nick: He is a hard worker?

Sue: You are right, we also have lots of evidence of how hard Brian works. Our job now is to use this evidence and say something about it. Nick told us that Brian is a hard worker. Looking at all the evidence we have about Brian's work ethic, what can we say about it?

(Sue gives the students time to think.)

Nick: He is a hard worker—I just said that.

Sue: Yes, I am asking you, all of you to go deeper, to say more. Think about it like this: Brian is a hard worker—so what? What does all this hard work tell you about Brian?

(Sue gives the students more time to reflect.)

Nick: Okay, now I have it. He is a hard worker, so he can survive.

Sue: What do you all think of this? Do you see how Brian's hard work is helping him survive?

Sarah: Yep, he didn't give up making a fire, and now he has fire and it's helping him live.

Sue: Exactly.

STEP 3 Interact with the text.

Sue: Now we have an idea to really explore. We know that Brian is a hard worker, and we know that this hard work is helping him in a big way. This knowledge is significant. Let's write it down.

(Sue jots this down in the class SmartNotes: *Brian is a hard worker. All his hard work helps him to survive.*)

Sue: As we keep reading, let's add to the evidence we have collected about the hard work Brian does that helps him survive. You are going to work with your independent reading thinking threads in a moment. Just like we've done here, your SmartNotes, going forward will focus on the thread you have chosen to develop.

STEP 4 Practice through independent work.

Sue: Your job is to pick a thread you noticed the other day in your independent reading, and say something about it. Then, like we just did, focus on adding evidence to that thread. Some of you will have a conference today, and everyone be ready to share your thinking at the end of the period.

STEP 5 Share.

(After 12 minutes, Sue gathers the class together and asks students to share.)

Jake: I'm reading *Hero* by Mike Lupica, and one thread I noticed was that Zach, the main character, wants to be independent.

Sue: Good start, Jake, now say something about Zach's independence. So what? Why does this matter?

Jake: He wants to be independent, but he can't because the problems he faces are too big.

Sue: Great. As you keep reading, follow that thread. Take SmartNotes about Zach's quest for independence.

Conclusion

Housing all their SmartNotes in a notebook means that students and teachers have a source of data that can be reread, re-visited, and reconsidered. The permanence of student thinking, conversation, and teacher instruction all stored in a SmartNote notebook is a beautiful thing: The data in the notebooks fosters student metacognition, teacher assessment, and planning of instruction.

In some classrooms, you see books peppered with small scraps of paper that record students' thinking. Although these sticky notes may be ubiquitous, they do little to move readers forward. These thoughts are disconnected, random, and left in the text without further reflection by students.

As the middle school student navigates a longer text, the thought thread that SmartNotes creates is crucial for deeper thought and analysis—and eventually writing about that thinking. Sticky notes just don't offer enough opportunity for reflection. The thinking recorded on them is fleeting, whereas SmartNotes display a definite track of student thinking.

CHAPTER FIVE

SmartNotes for Levels of Comprehension

Middle school classrooms are diverse communities. Everyone is reading something different and thinking at different levels, so the SmartNotes that students in your class take will look different from one another. Again, the power of SmartNotes is their flexibility. The thinking shown in students' SmartNotes reflects their level of comprehension and depth of thought, giving you the opportunity to identify that level of comprehension and then to tailor your instruction to each learner.

Knowing the students in front of you is the name of the game. SmartNotes give you the ability to identify students' capacity for thinking and their comfort with strategies, and evaluate their comprehension. SmartNotes and the CCSS support one another; it's a no-brainer. The Common Core is a rigorous set of standards. Students can no longer hide behind literal responses; they must be able to make inferences, support claims, and reflect their understanding through writing.

Fountas and Pinnell, the pioneers of leveled libraries, have inspired teachers to truly understand comprehension. They have unpacked "comprehension," and in their tome, *Continuum of Literacy Learning* (2010), have identified three levels of comprehension:

- Within-the-text
- Beyond-the-text
- About-the-text

Understanding that comprehension is not static, nor black and white, helps teachers support thinkers to fully grasp the ideas presented in the texts they read. The Common Core State Standards expect students to be able to tap into all three levels of comprehension, moving fluidly through the levels as needed. Below, we explain the three levels through the lens of SmartNotes.

Within-the-Text Comprehension

Comprehension at this level is literal. Students are asked to identify specific information in the text, such as the following:

- *What is the problem?*
- *What is happening?*
- *What do you know so far?*
- *When does this event take place?*
- *Who/what is involved?*
- *What are the characters doing?*

To respond to these types of questions, readers must be able to pull information from the text. This information is right there on the page. When students retell or summarize text, they use this level of comprehension. This level of comprehension is what allows students to find text details to support a claim.

SMARTNOTES

When we launch SmartNotes, all the thinking that students record is at this level. Students are asked to notice who, what, when, and where—the basics—about their text. This is what within-the-text thinking is all about. Students identify important information that helps them get a handle on the text. Recording details from the text in SmartNotes makes the deeper thinking easier.

CONFERENCES

The comprehension of struggling readers is often at this within-the-text level. Getting them to understand a text, even at this literal level, can be a challenge. These students have difficulty choosing the right information/detail to record in a SmartNote. Sifting through all the information in the text can be overwhelming to them. For students at this level of comprehension, helping them figure out what is important in a text is the goal of a conference.

SAMPLE CONFERENCE

Lisa, a fifth grader, is reading The Lightning Thief *by Rick Riordan. Lisa is the kind of reader who is fully capable of reading every word, but she doesn't know which details to focus on—which details are important.*

Sue: Show me your SmartNotes.

Lisa: Well, I just read up to the middle of page 174 when you came over.

Sue: Okay, sorry, I will get you back to reading shortly. So show me your SmartNotes.

Lisa: (reads) "Percy is hungry, he wants Auntie Em's burgers."

Sue: Show me where this happened on page 174.

(Lisa points to where the information appears on the page.)

Sue: Remember, when you take SmartNotes, it is important to write the exact words from the text along with your thinking. Let's do it together.

[Lisa writes: "Go ahead, call me an idiot for walking into a strange lady's shop just like that because I was hungry, but I do impulsive stuff sometimes." (p. 174)]

Sue: Good. Percy is hungry. Talk to me about why you found this information important.

Lisa: Well, he and his friends have not eaten in awhile, and they found this place and it looked good.

Sue: Out of everything you just read on page 174 about Auntie Em's Garden Gnome Emporium, is Percy's being hungry the most important part?

(Lisa looks confused. She avoids eye contact with Sue. This tells Sue that Lisa clearly doesn't understand the question.)

Sue: Let's think about this. Let's focus on the quote you chose—it's a good one. We learned that Percy was hungry, but what else did we learn?

Lisa: It also says Percy does impulsive stuff.

Sue: Yes—what do you think that means?

 Independent Reading in the Age of Common Core © 2013 by Sue Cannone-Calick & Elizabeth Henley • Scholastic Teaching Resources

Lisa: Umm, I think it means that he just does stuff—like he doesn't think.

Sue: Exactly. So let's think about what we know: Percy is hungry and wanders into the first place he finds without thinking. Is this a good idea?

Lisa: Well, umm, I don't know. On 174 it also says that Grover, his friend, was nervous.

Sue: Excellent: Grover is nervous, and Percy is impulsive—not thinking things through. So what do you think now? Is going into this place a good idea?

Lisa: Umm. Not really?

Sue: Yes. Rick Riordan writes that Percy is hungry but impulsive—the impulsive part is really important. So what is really important here is that Percy might be making a bad decision all because he is hungry. Let's add that to your SmartNotes.

(Lisa adds her thinking to her SmartNotes. The complete SmartNote appears below.)

"Go ahead, call me an idiot for walking into a strange lady's shop just like that because I was hungry, but I do impulsive stuff sometimes." (p. 174) *Percy is hungry, but not thinking through everything. Eating here might not be a good idea.*

Sue: Good SmartNote. Your task is to write down only the important information from the text. Just like we did today, think it through: ask yourself why the information is important.

Debrief: Lisa was thinking very literally. Her initial SmartNote only contained basic information. Noticing Percy was hungry was fine, but she missed the important information that Percy was impulsive and that Grover's hesitation meant the place was not safe. Summary SmartNotes are literal, but they should reflect the important text information.

Sue needed to push Lisa to think more deeply about the text. This SmartNote was a combination of both Lisa's and Sue's thinking. Heavily supporting student thinking in this way is okay because it shows learners how to think more deeply, but eventually we want Lisa to independently determine what is important.

Beyond-the-Text Comprehension

This level of comprehension requires students to take the information they learned in a text and apply their thinking to it. In other words, they need to add their thoughts to the text. Being *able* to apply a reading strategy is beyond-the-text thinking. *Writing* that thinking creates a SmartNote. When students predict, connect, visualize, and infer, they are thinking beyond the text. When they record all that thinking, they are SmartNoting. The CCSS values thinking beyond the literal.

SMARTNOTES

SmartNotes taken at this level are more complex. Students record information from the text and then reflect on it. This reflection is an opportunity to show in writing that they understand what they read and how they arrived at that understanding. Taking SmartNotes at this level is effective because students show what they know. It isn't enough that beyond-the-text thinkers effectively use a reading strategy; they have to know how they used a strategy and why it is important in their reading to use it at that moment.

CONFERENCES

Readers at this level know what is important in their reading and are ready to start considering how their thinking helps them interact with and understand the text better. While students may know that they made a connection or prediction after reading their text, they also need to know how using those strategies will help them go beyond the surface to understand plot, character, content, sequence, cause and effect, and theme at a smarter, deeper level.

Let's go back to the conference with Lisa about *The Lightning Thief* on page 86. Sue pushed Lisa to see the danger of Percy's going into Auntie Em's Burgers. Had Lisa been able to identify this on her own, Sue's next step would have been to encourage beyond-the-text thinking. For example, knowing that Percy is impulsive and that Grover is nervous about the place, Lisa would have been able to predict that something bad was going to happen there. The conference would have then focused on how that prediction helped Lisa understand the plot and the direction (lots of harrowing escapes from danger) the author is going in.

SAMPLE CONFERENCE

Chris is a typical seventh grader who is reading The Outsiders *by S. E. Hinton.*

Betsy: Show me your SmartNotes, Chris.

Chris: (reads) Page 98: "He was stroking my hair and I could hear the sobs racking him as he fought to keep back the tears. Oh, Pony, I thought we'd lost you . . . like we did Mom and Dad."

> *Ponyboy finally understands Darry. He realizes that Darry loves him.*

Betsy: Talk to me about this. Tell me about the relationship Ponyboy has with Darry.

Chris: Well, they used to have a really tough relationship. Darry was really hard on Pony and even hit him. That is why Ponyboy ran away. Now that Ponyboy is back with Darry, he sees how much Darry missed him and loved him.

Betsy: This is really good thinking. How does Ponyboy figure all this out about Darry?

Chris: Ponyboy just almost died and I think he was happy to see Darry even though he had been so mad at him before he left. He probably wasn't expecting Darry to cry.

Betsy: Okay. You now have proof that Darry loves Ponyboy. What does this help you understand about their relationship? Think back to the beginning of the book.

Chris: Oh, no wonder Darry was so hard on Pony. It's like he really was trying to be Pony's dad.

Betsy: Yes—exactly! You took an excellent SmartNote. It helped you understand what you read. Your job is to use that thinking to understand other parts of the book. Think about what you now know about Darry. Has your thinking about him changed? Explain.

Chris: (pauses to think) I used to think that Darry was awful. He was mean to Pony—Pony even said so. Now, I think Darry was trying to protect Pony and maybe yelling at him was the only thing he knew how to do.

Betsy: You are great. That was fabulous. You used your new knowledge of Darry to reflect back and see him differently. Now, you understand Darry in a way you didn't before. Your task: Continue to use what you learn about the characters to think back to understand them better or differently.

Debrief: Chris clearly understood what he read. He chose a good part of the text to think about, and he was able to go beyond the text and make inferences about a character. For a student who is able to do this level of thinking, it is the teacher's job to push him still further. Betsy helped Chris take the smart thinking he did and use it to get a deeper understanding of a character. Now Chris knows how to extend an inference and apply it to the larger text. Proficient readers do this automatically; Betsy has modeled this thinking for Chris so he will soon be able to do this independently.

About-the-Text Comprehension

This thinking requires readers to use what they know about text structure to get a fuller understanding of the story: What did the author do to help you, the reader, really understand the text? This could include noticing narration, point of view, chapter length, use of literary devices, word choice, nonfiction text features, or complex text structure. Clear examples of this would be when an author uses flashbacks or foreshadowing, when a story is embedded within another story (as in *Holes* by Louis Sachar, *Walk Two Moons* by Sharon Creech, and *Bomb: The Race to Build—and Steal—the World's Most Dangerous Weapon* by Steve Sheinkin) or when a text is written in letter or diary form (for example, *Catherine Called Birdy* by Karen Cushman and *P. S. Longer Letter Later* by Paula Danziger and Ann M. Martin). Text structure standards are at the front and center of the Common Core.

SMARTNOTES

Pointing out text structure to a student is important. Some students notice these nuances in a text, while others cannot. Sophisticated readers have the ability to sift through and pick out elements from a text. In this case, their SmartNotes indicate these observations; however, students must ultimately question how noticing the elements will help them understand the text better. As with the beyond-the-text thinking we discussed with Chris's conference, just noticing isn't enough. When students do not seem aware of text structure, it is apparent from their SmartNotes. For these readers, as we did with Lisa, we would provide the structural element and help them think about its significance. Proficient readers are able to find the element and only need nudging to understand its significance.

CONFERENCES

About-the-text conferences require students to look at a text as a whole—noticing what the author does to the text. This means paying attention to structure, for example, alternating narrators, diary format, letters and/or playing with time structures. This thinking encourages students to step away from the words themselves and analyze how the author presents information.

SAMPLE CONFERENCE

Madeleine, a typical seventh grader, is reading Flipped *by Wendelin Van Draanen.*

Betsy: Show me your SmartNotes.

Madeleine: As I was reading, I got confused. When the story started, I noticed a boy, Bryce, was telling the story. Then when I got to the next chapter, I wrote, "The first day I met Bryce Loski, I flipped." (p. 11). I wrote a question: *I thought Bryce was telling the story?*

Betsy: Good question. Talk me through your confusion.

Madeleine: Let's see. I kept reading and saw that now a girl, Julianna, was telling the story.

Betsy: Exactly, how did you know?

Madeleine: Her name is written at the bottom of her pages.

Betsy: Go back to the other chapter. What do you notice?

Madeleine: Ahhh, Bryce's name is at the top.

Betsy: So now tell me: How is this book organized?

Madeleine: The author switches back and forth between the two narrators. Is that why the title is *Flipped*?

Betsy: Good guess. Hold onto that thought. Now that you know Wendelin Van Draanen will be alternating between narrators, the question is why do you think she would do that?

Madeleine: Let me think. I already noticed that when Julianna started her story, it was some of the same stuff that Bryce talked about in his story. It was the same story, but from her side.

Betsy: Great. Van Draanen tells the same story but switches perspective. How do you think this will help you understand the story?

Madeleine: Well, I think I am going to get her story and his story.

Betsy: Yes, that makes sense. Here is something to think about, Madeleine: Whose story do you believe?

Madeleine: I don't know.

Betsy: That is a good thing for you to think about: Whose story is more truthful? As you read, keep in mind that Van Draanen did this on purpose so you can figure out something about these two characters. Your task is to keep this in mind as you read. Your observations should be in your SmartNotes.

Madeleine: Okay, I will!

Debrief: Madeleine is a proficient, capable, and excited reader. This is evident from her SmartNotes and her ability to talk about her thinking. She is the ideal "About-the-Text" thinker. She noticed on her own that the author switched narrators and was excited with very little prompting to think about its significance. This level of thinking is difficult and usually requires more prompting from the teacher. That is okay. It is important for readers to pay attention to text structure, and they often need a push to do this.

Because about-the-text thinking is a challenge for many students, it should initially be taught as a whole-class mini-lesson rather than in a one-to-one conference.

About-the-Text Thinking
SmartNotes Mini-Lesson

CCSS RI.5.5, RI.6.5, RI.7.5, RI.8.5

MATERIALS

- Mentor texts: *The American Plague: The True and Terrifying Story of the Yellow Fever Epidemic of 1793* by Jim Murphy and *Flesh and Blood So Cheap* by Albert Marrin (teacher copy and one copy for each student)
- Chart paper or whiteboard (dry-erase or interactive) and markers
- Student notebooks and pencils

STEP 1 Explain the purpose of instruction.

This lesson will tackle text structure within nonfiction texts. Traditionally, nonfiction books were organized in chronological order, and readers were prepared for this. Now, readers have to be able to identify different structures such as cause/effect and problem/solution. Students need to learn to understand these structures, why the author set up the information this way, and how to use the structure to better understand the text. This lesson requires students to notice the structure of two texts and to compare and contrast those structures, as well as how those structures provide them with information.

STEP 2 Demonstrate the strategy in action.

(Over the past few days, Betsy has read aloud the first three chapters of *An American Plague*. We have been working on noticing text structure.)

Betsy: Yesterday we finished chapter three of *An American Plague*, and we talked about how the book didn't sound like nonfiction, it sounded like a story, and what Jim Murphy did to make it sound that way for his readers. Yesterday, our discussion was about how Murphy started the text before the fever broke out and presented the information chronologically. As a result, we learned about Philadelphia and the fever as it happened—no spoilers or advanced information. This structure leaves readers learning events as they unfold.

Today, we are going to read the beginning of a different nonfiction text, *Flesh and Blood So Cheap*, which is about the Triangle Factory fire in New York City in the early 1900s. Our focus will be to notice the different structure this author, Albert Marrin, uses.

STEP 3 Interact with the text.

(Betsy reads the first two pages, the prelude, of *Flesh and Blood So Cheap*.)

Betsy: What do readers learn right away?

John: There was a fire and 146 people died.

Betsy: Yes, let's make a SmartNote.

(Betsy writes on the board: Flesh and Blood So Cheap *starts off with telling us there is a tragic fire where 146 people died.*)

Betsy: In *An American Plague*, I didn't find out about the epidemic until the end. Here, I know the end, and I just read the prologue. I wonder why the authors chose to organize their texts in these different ways.

Let's analyze these two texts. *American Plague* is chronological—readers learn the information in the order that it happened. BUT . . . in *Flesh and Blood*, readers learn about the big event at the beginning. Let's compare the organization of these texts. What is good about each of these two different structures?

(Betsy gives students a few minutes to think.)

Betsy: Say something.

Sean: This book started at the end, so we already know about the fire.

Jessica: Yes, and Murphy's book hasn't gotten to the bad stuff yet.

Betsy: Let's get this clear, so we can write a SmartNote. *American Plague* is organized in a chronological way—in time order—while the information in *Flesh and Blood So Cheap* is given in chunks, giving readers information at different times.

(Betsy writes this on the board and then gives students time to copy the SmartNote into their notebooks.)

Betsy: This is important because as readers, we can expect different things from these two books. We can expect Murphy in *American Plague* to slowly unfurl the story—piece by piece as it happens. On the other hand, we can't expect that from Marrin. Why would Murphy and Marrin choose to structure their texts in these ways?

Jessica: I want to finish reading both texts.

Betsy: Why?

Jessica: Because I am so interested to find out about the fire and to know the rest of the plague saga.

Betsy: Both authors did a good job reeling you in. Why would an author like Marrin choose to give away the important part so early?

Sam: He wants us to keep reading?

Betsy: Now let's all go back to the structure SmartNote we just took and add the reason why text structure is so important.

(Betsy adds the following to the SmartNote, while students copy it into their notebooks.)

> *American Plague is organized in a chronological way—in time order—while the information in Flesh and Blood So Cheap is given in chunks, giving readers information at different times. Chronological order helps readers know the story as it happens, while telling the end first, makes readers want to know the specific details. Both authors get readers interested.*

STEP 4 Practice through independent reading.

Betsy: When you start reading your independent nonfiction text, pay attention in your SmartNotes to the choice the author makes about presenting information. We will ask some of you to share at the end of IR.

(Betsy sends students off to read as she and Sue have independent conferences.)

 **STEP 5** **Share.**

(After 12 minutes, Betsy calls the class together to share their thoughts.)

Mary: I am reading *Amelia Lost* and the author, Candace Fleming, organizes the text kind of like *Flesh and Blood So Cheap*, so I know from the beginning that Amelia Earhart disappears.

Betsy: Great work, Mary. Keep reading to see how Fleming presents information throughout the text.

Conclusion

Many students start at the within-the-text level of comprehension, and it is a gradual process to achieve deeper understanding, although not necessarily a linear one. There are times when all readers will choose to be within-the-text thinkers—for example, when reading a textbook or directions in a manual. Even though some students may be literal thinkers and still need help with within-the-text level thinking, do not limit them to this level. To progress, they need to be exposed to all levels of thinking.

As teachers, you should be able to monitor the amount of time each student dips into the various levels of comprehension and how long they spend there. If you notice that a student's SmartNotes are always at the within-the-text level, it is important to record this and do some further investigating; maybe he or she is reading texts that are too hard. It is important that you can recognize students' level of comprehension so you can move them along and ensure that their thinking grows; it is not necessary, however, to label the level for the student.

CHAPTER SIX

Using SmartNotes to Write About Reading

The Common Core State Standards require students to write about reading, and to use text evidence to support their claims. SmartNotes offer a fresh perspective on how to get students to write about their reading in a smart, focused, and clear way. SmartNotes are not an end in themselves; they help students support an idea they have been thinking about from the text and/ or lead them to making a big idea/thesis statement.

SmartNotes as Support

There is more required of readers than simply enjoying a text. Readers, as we have talked about, must think through the text, come up with original ideas about it, and prove these ideas/support a claim with evidence from the text. This is the basis of analytical writing.

In elementary school, readers are often asked to write about reading. These responses are usually written in a personal voice; students comment on what they liked about a text. At the middle school level, students' responses to their reading take on a more authoritative voice— personal pronouns are gone, and students must have evidence to support their ideas. SmartNotes provide the evidence needed for this analytical writing.

Writing about reading is one way for students to show what they know about a text. Well-rounded students are familiar with many forms of writing about reading. Some writing is informal and uses a casual, personal voice; formal writing is analytical and has an authoritative tone.

LITERARY LETTERS: AN INFORMAL APPROACH

Literary letters are a staple in our curriculum. In *In the Middle* (1998), Nancie Atwell describes literary letters as a way for readers to write about their reading; in Atwell's class, the letters are a back-and-forth dialogue between the teacher and student. The conversation is free flowing and loosely structured. This informal dialogue encourages students to voice their opinions, reflect on the text, and produce a thoughtful text analysis. Our version of literary letters, on the other hand, has a structure that focuses on SmartNotes as the central piece of reflection and support.

In our Literary Letter Assignment, students are required to expand on a few of their SmartNotes (page 115). A Literary Letter Assignment organizer has space for five paragraphs, but this assignment can be modified to fit the needs of your students.

- The first paragraph is similar to an introduction. It asks for title, author, genre, where the reader is in the text, and a brief summary.

- The next three paragraphs, similar to body paragraphs, require one SmartNote each—a quote, student thinking and a So What? Students select the SmartNotes to include. This independent choice is important because it shows students' metacognition: they must pick the right SmartNotes—the ones that they have enough to say about and that can back up their thinking.

- Since this is an informal piece, students' voice is vital; the final paragraph is a recommendation. Students think about friends in their literary community who would enjoy the text or who should be warned that it is not a worthwhile read.

We create an exemplar model letter with the class text, and then students write letters based on their independent reading book. Two exemplar model letters appear at the right. The first exemplar uses *Hatchet* by Gary Paulsen. The second one uses a biography of John F. Kennedy, *Who Was John F. Kennedy?* by Yona Zeldis McDonough.

Again, the informal quality of this writing allows the student's personality to come through. The use of first-person narration encourages readers to share their personal point of view, perspective, and opinion. The SmartNotes we refer to in the exemplars are the ones students found memorable; students remembered the SmartNotes because they understood them, and as a result, writing about these SmartNotes is easy.

Knowing what is required in the letter, students start by culling their SmartNotes, looking for memorable and interesting ideas they want to share with us. Then they complete the Letter Assignment organizer and handwrite a rough draft. At this point, we have a conference with each student focusing on the ideas in each SmartNote and talking through the So What? The letter is then either typed or handwritten for publication.

Dear Ms. Cannone and Ms. Henley,

Right now I am reading <u>Hatchet</u> by Gary Paulsen. It has been incredibly exciting so far. I am not even half way through yet, so I am eager to read what adventures come next. Brian, the main character, has been in a plane accident. The pilot, who was flying him to visit his dad, had a heart attack. Brian was left to fly the plane on his own. Amazingly, he lands the plane in a lake and survives.

Brian is brave. From the moment he realizes that it is up to him to land the plane and decides that he isn't going to give up—"He had to fly it somehow. Had to fly the plane"(15), to when he takes stock of everything around him, "I am Brian Robeson. I have been in a plane crash. I am going to find some food. I am going to find berries"(63)—Brian stays strong. Most people I know, including me, would get really freaked out and just cry if they were in a situation like Brian is. I am really impressed that he was able to dig deep into himself and find courage the way he did; it couldn't have been easy.

Another thought I had while reading this book is that Brian stays positive. If I were in his situation I would not be handling things so smoothly. I think my fears about being alone would probably stop me from being able to think. Brian isn't that way though. He stays focused on what he needs to do, " I have to get motivated... he had to do something to help himself"(51). This kind of drive is cool to see, especially in someone so young.

Reading <u>Hatchet</u> is very different than lots of other books I have read. There are things in this book that are gross. Brian throws up a lot, gets attacked by mosquitoes and is sunburned all over his face. Gary Paulsen writes in a really detailed way that makes me say "ugh" a lot. I guess he does that so the people who read the book really get what Brian's life is like.

If you are like me, and enjoy reading about a real kid in a real situation, you will like this book. Something about the way Brian deals with what happens to him is inspirational. I want to keep reading to see what happens and how things go for him.

Dear Ms. Cannone and Ms. Henley,

I am reading *Who Was John F. Kennedy?*, by Yona Zeldis McDonough. Kennedy was from Boston, Massachusetts from a rich, Catholic family. He had many brothers and sisters. His father encouraged him to work hard and eventually go into politics. Kennedy became President of the United States in 1960.

One character trait inference I made was that John F. Kennedy was brave. He was a sailor in the U.S. Navy during World War II, commanding the boat, PT109, a patrol boat in the Pacific Ocean. During a night-time mission his boat was attacked by a Japanese destroyer. The boat was sinking. He ordered his men to abandon the ship and swim to safety. One sailor, Patrick McMahon, was badly burned and could not swim. The author writes, "Jack refused to leave Patrick McMahon, who was badly burned to die alone. Instead, he placed Patrick on top of him, back to back" (36). Kennedy risked his life taking care of someone else. While under attack, it must have been extra challenging to swim with another person on his back. Putting others before himself, John F. Kennedy's valiant effort to bring Patrick home is exactly the quality Americans want in their Commander in Chief.

John F. Kennedy's motivational quality moved the Nation. Americans looked to John F. Kennedy for strength, hope, faith and confidence. He encouraged Americans to step up and take care of those less fortunate, "JFK also created the Peace Corp. Young men and women volunteered to spend two years in a needy country where they helped build schools, water wells, health centers and other projects"(82). This spirit of giving was inspirational, another quality Americans look for in their president.

John F. Kennedy of one of the most important and popular presidents. He was famous as the first Catholic president, but more importantly he energized America. Americans wanted to connect to this young, attractive family man. He was a civil rights leader, a forward thinking man who got us to space! Standing tough against bullies, JFK proved to the world that America was force to be reckoned with.

Fondly,

FREEWRITING

Writing about reading does not always need a structure. Sometimes it is beneficial to have students reflect on their SmartNotes without having to write a formal paragraph. Freewriting encourages students to put all their thinking down on paper. This exploration of thought can lead to further writing: letters, paragraphs, or a thesis statement. Here are some prompts we've used to jumpstart freewriting assignments:

- *We have spent so much time thinking about Sal and Phoebe in* Walk Two Moons. *Use the SmartNotes you have taken about them to think about their relationship. What do you think of Sal and Phoebe as people? What do you think of their relationship with each other?*

- *We have noticed that E. L. Konigsburg uses punctuation in interesting ways throughout* The View from Saturday. *What do you notice about her writing style? How does Konigsburg's use of semi-colons, dashes, and commas help you as a reader?*

- Catherine, Called Birdy *is written as a diary. What do you think about this?*

- *As we read* Sign of the Beaver, *we have talked about the role of setting in this book. What do you think about the setting?*

- *Jonas's community in* The Giver *has many rules. What do you think about this?*

Many of these informal tasks ask students to write what they think. Giving them an open forum for their thoughts—using their SmartNotes—is invaluable. The fact that there is no right answer encourages out-of-the-box thinking and reaffirms students' good thinking. All these ideas came from the thinking around our class text. Then we ask students to take a thread from their own independent reading SmartNotes and reflect on it.

USING SMARTNOTES TO WRITE AN ANALYTICAL PARAGRAPH

Informal writing is a good tool to use to assess student understanding of the text and their use of SmartNotes. Analytical paragraphs, on the other hand, are more structured and get at students' ability to use a text in order to prove an idea (in Grades 5 and 6) and eventually a thesis (Grades 7 and 8). The Common Core requires this work; claims must be supported, and thinking validated. This kind of writing is essential for students as they move through middle school and into high school toward college readiness. These analytical paragraphs are the stepping stones to writing essays, lab reports, and research papers.

SmartNotes are text plus thinking. Taking SmartNotes promotes inferential thinking and supports paragraph writing. SmartNotes are the foundation of these paragraphs; they provide the evidence that supports students' inferences. As shown below, a paragraph at the analytical level contains a topic sentence and three connected ideas, each of which builds off the prior one so each step reflects deeper analytical thinking.

- Topic sentence: What inference am I trying to prove in this paragraph?

- A sentence that answers this question: What more can I say about the inference in my topic sentence?

- A sentence or sentences that answer this question: What background information do I need to give the reader about the quote in the SmartNote?

- A quote that answers this question: Which quote best proves the inference in my topic sentence?

- Sentences that answer this question: How can I explain/analyze the quote to show that it proves my inference? (This is the So What?)

- Clincher: How can I sum up my thinking?

Formal, analytical writing is new to fifth graders, so we provide students with an Analytical Paragraph Organizer (page 116) to help support their thinking. Additionally, we write an analytical paragraph together with students, using our core text, as shown in the mini-lesson below. This exemplar is a good jumping off point for students' independent work.

Character Trait Analytical Paragraph SmartNote Mini-Lesson

The series of skills involved in using SmartNotes to write an analytical paragraph requires five days of lessons. This is not a traditional mini-lesson where students practice through reading and writing about their independent reading book. All the practice that students do in this mini-lesson is centered around our class text.

 W.5.1, W.5.2, W.5.8, W.6.1, W.6.2, W.6.8, W.7.1, W.7.2, W.7.8, W.8.1, W.8.2, W.8.8

MATERIALS
- Mentor text: *Walk Two Moons* by Sharon Creech (teacher copy and one for each student)
- Character Trait Web (completed in class the day before: see page 98)
- Analytical Paragraph Organizer (one for each student: see page 116)
- Chart paper or whiteboard (dry-erase or interactive) and markers
- Student notebooks and pens or pencils

DAY 1: CHOOSING A TOPIC

STEP 1 Explain the purpose of instruction.

Identifying a character trait and supporting it with text evidence makes a good first analytical paragraph. Teaching students how to express themselves analytically is an important step in middle school. Using a text students know well and a character they care about makes the process of analyzing easier.

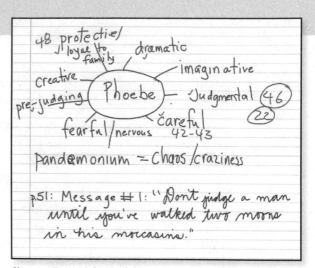

Character Trait Web for Phoebe

(We have been reading *Walk Two Moons* by Sharon Creech and noticing character traits. Betsy displays the class SmartNotes for the text and the Character Trait Web for Phoebe completed in class in the previous lesson.)

Betsy: Yesterday, we made this web about Phoebe's character traits. We came up with many adjectives that describe her personality.

Today, we are going to choose one trait to write about in a paragraph. We are going to be writing what is called an analytical paragraph. It is a little different than the paragraphs you wrote in elementary school. When you were in fourth grade, you had to use details that proved your main idea or topic sentence, but now, the details you use will come from a text, and you have to prove the thinking you do around that text.

Over the next few days, we are going to write an analytical paragraph together about one of Phoebe's character traits. Then you are going to write one on your own about another of Phoebe's character traits. Today, I am going to focus on Phoebe's being convincing. I am going to go back through our SmartNotes to find notes we took about this character trait. I'd like you to look through the class SmartNotes you took, too.

(Betsy scrolls through class SmartNotes as students look through their notebooks.)

STEP 2 Demonstrate the strategy in action.

Betsy: Here is a SmartNote from page 23:

"Do you want to know an absolute secret?' Phoebe said. . . .'Her name is Mrs. Cadaver, right? Have you ever wondered what happened to Mr. Cadaver?'" *Phoebe is so dramatic she is convincing Sal that something is wrong with Mrs. Cadaver. She raises questions about Mrs. Cadaver that neither one of them can really answer. She convinces Sal to think badly of Mrs. Cadaver as well.*

This SmartNote allows us to infer that Phoebe is a convincing person—she knows how to make Sal feel the same way about Mrs. Cadaver as she does. That is Phoebe's power.

STEP 3 Interact with text.

Betsy: Take a look again at our Character Trait Web for Phoebe. Choose a trait you want to write about and prove with text and SmartNote support. Work with the person next to you to find a SmartNote to support the trait you each want to focus on.
(Betsy walks around to support partners as they sift through their SmartNotes. She gives them 12 minutes to find a trait and write a SmartNote that backs it up.)

Betsy: What trait were you trying to prove, John?

John: Dramatic. Olivia and I found a SmartNote from page forty-three.

Betsy: Everyone, turn to your SmartNotes from page forty-three. John, what's the quote?

John: "Maybe he has a knife tucked into his socks."

Betsy: What thinking had we added to that quote?

John: We wrote: *Phoebe is really taking this to the next level and acting irrational.*

Betsy: Can you all see how this quote proves that Phoebe is dramatic? (Students nod in agreement.) Tomorrow, we will pick up here and continue proving the character trait.

DAY 2: WRITING A TOPIC SENTENCE

STEP 1 Explain the purpose of instruction.

This is a continuation of Day 1's work. Today, we are building off the quote students picked and filling out an Analytical Paragraph Organizer that supports the trait.

(Sue opens class by reviewing the character trait assigned to Phoebe and the quote that proves the trait from the previous day's lesson.)

Sue: Open your notebooks to yesterday's work; the Phoebe trait and the quote that proves that trait. Yesterday, we worked through a SmartNote proving that Phoebe is convincing. Today, we will start writing our analytical paragraph on that topic. This organizer will help us do that.

(Sue distributes a copy of the Analytical Paragraph Organizer to each student and displays a copy of it.)

STEP 2 Demonstrate the strategy in action.

Sue: Let's look at the components of an analytical paragraph shown on the organizer. There are six parts to the paragraph.

(Sue reads the six sections of the organizer aloud.)

Sue: Yesterday, you found two parts of the paragraph without even knowing it. First, you chose a Phoebe trait to concentrate on. This information will go in the first box of the organizer. Then, you found the quote. This information will eventually go in the fourth box.

Topic Sentence: What inference am I trying to prove in this paragraph?

In my example from yesterday, I focused on Phoebe's being convincing. I can't just write Phoebe is convincing—there is more to a topic sentence than that. We need readers to know who Phoebe is and where this character is from. I am going to introduce Phoebe by mentioning the title and author of the book she appears in. Here is my topic sentence:

Phoebe, Sal's friend from Walk Two Moons *by Sharon Creech, is a very convincing person.*

STEP 3 Interact with the text.

Sue: Let's have one of you volunteer to try out a topic sentence for the trait you chose.

Gabby: Phoebe, in *Walk Two Moons* by Sharon Creech, is dramatic.

STEP 4 Practice through independent work.

Sue: Excellent. Now everyone try. Write a topic sentence that mentions the title, author, and trait you will prove. Write it in the Topic Sentence box on the organizer.

(For 5 minutes, Sue walks around the room to observe and provide assistance as students write a topic sentence.)

Sue: Great job. Tomorrow we will continue with this paragraph.

DAY 3: SAYING MORE ABOUT THE INFERENCE

STEP 1 Explain the purpose of instruction.

This is a continuation of Day 2's work. Today, we are building off the topic sentence students wrote and adding more explanation to the trait.

Betsy: Yesterday you all wrote a topic sentence that introduced your readers to the trait you are going to prove. Today, we are continuing with the organizer and moving on to the sentence where you say more about the trait.

STEP 2 Demonstrate the strategy in action.

Betsy: In the class example, I wrote that Phoebe was convincing. Why is that true? What makes her convincing? When you are completing the second section of the Analytical Paragraph Organizer, ask yourself: *Why is this trait true?* You aren't using a quote from your SmartNotes yet, you are explaining the trait. Let me think out loud for you:

What does it mean to be convincing? A person who is convincing makes people believe what they believe. To be convincing means you have a way with words so you can persuade people to agree with you. In the second section of the organizer, I will write a general statement defining and explaining the trait:

A sentence that answers this question: **What more can I say** about the inference in my topic sentence?

Here is what I will write in the second box: *She is able to get Sal to believe what she believes and agree with her.*

STEP 3 Interact with the text.

Betsy: Your job now is to try to write this sentence for the trait you are working on. Who wants to try it out loud?

Max: I'm doing imaginative. I would write: Phoebe likes to make believe things.

Betsy: Excellent. Making believe is another way of saying how imaginative Phoebe is.

STEP 4 Practice through independent work.

Betsy: Everyone is going to try it now. Write a sentence that explains/defines the trait you chose. (For about five minutes, Betsy walks around and checks sentences.)

Betsy: Good work today. Tomorrow we will work through the next three sections of the organizer.

DAY 4: WRITING THE BODY

STEP 1 Explain the purpose of instruction.

This is a continuation of Day 3's work. Today, we'll write the bulk of the analytical paragraph where we use a SmartNote quote to prove the character trait inference.

Sue: Today we are going to work through the bulk of the paragraph. We are really going to prove and explain the inference we made about the Phoebe character trait. Take a look at the next three sections of the organizer. The third section provides background information and prepares the reader for the quote—which leads directly to the quote you have already selected—and finally, you must explain or analyze the quote to show how it proves the trait /inference.

(Sue pulls up the partly completed organizer on the interactive whiteboard.)

Our class analytical paragraph is about Phoebe being convincing. The question I need to ask myself is "What would someone need to know about Phoebe and the events of the story to understand how she is convincing?" Let me think this through: Phoebe has definite and negative opinions about her neighbor, Mrs. Cadaver. Phoebe believes that Mrs. Cadaver is evil, a diabolical person. These assumptions are far-fetched.

STEP 2 **Demonstrate the strategy in action.**

Sue: For the third section about background information on the Analytical Paragraph Organizer, I will write:

Phoebe doesn't trust her neighbor, Mrs. Cadaver, thinking she is a diabolical person. She shares her negative opinions with Sal.

The quote goes in the next section. We have already chosen a quote, and it should flow nicely from the background sentence you just wrote. Our class quote is this:

"'Do you want to know an absolute secret?' Phoebe said. . . . 'Her name is Mrs. Cadaver, right? Have you ever wondered what happened to Mr. Cadaver?'"

This works well because the background information leads us right to the words from the text.

The next section is the explanation. It is our job to explain how the quote proves the trait/inference from the topic sentence. To do this part, we must go back to our thinking in the SmartNote. Our thinking in the SmartNote already proves the inference. Having the So What? in your SmartNote makes writing an analytical paragraph a lot easier—you have already done the smart/analytical thinking. The thinking we had with the quote is here in our SmartNotes:

Phoebe is so dramatic she is convincing Sal that something is wrong with Mrs. Cadaver. She raises questions about Mrs. Cadaver that neither one of them can really answer. She convinces Sal to think badly of Mrs. Cadaver just like she does.

Now we have to put the three sections together. Here are the three sections we just worked through:

Phoebe doesn't trust her neighbor, Mrs. Cadaver, thinking she is a diabolical person. She tells Sal about her negative opinions. "'Do you want to know an absolute secret?' Phoebe said. . . . 'Her name is Mrs. Cadaver, right? Have you ever wondered what happened to Mr. Cadaver?'" (p. 23). Phoebe is so dramatic she is convincing Sal that something is wrong with Mrs. Cadaver. She raises questions about Mrs. Cadaver that neither one of them can really answer. She convinces Sal to think badly of Mrs. Cadaver just like she does.

(There is no Step 3 on Day 4 as the modeling leads directly to independent work.)

STEP 4 **Practice through independent work.**

Sue: This requires thought, but you are ready to try this. Your job is to fill in the next three sections on the Analytical Paragraph Organizer for the Phoebe trait you are proving. Use our class sample to help you. I will walk around to help.

(Students work as Sue walks around to assist. Sue gives them about 20 minutes to work.)

Sue: Good work. Tomorrow, we will finish the organizer!

DAY 5: WRITING THE CONCLUSION

STEP 1 • Explain the purpose of instruction.

This is the final day of the paragraph work. Today, students write the conclusion sentence, which sums up the idea presented in the topic sentence and further extends the idea.

Betsy: Take a look at everything you have written so far about the character in your independent reading book. I will read aloud what we have for our class example.

(Betsy reads the paragraph as it stands.)

So far, we have identified the character's trait, given background information, set up the quote, provided the quote, and given a thorough "So What?" to explain how the quote proves the trait. Read your paragraph to make sure you have all those parts, too.

(Betsy waits while students read their work.)

Today, we will finish our paragraph by writing a conclusion sentence.

STEP 2 • Demonstrate the strategy in action.

Betsy: The conclusion sentence sums up the whole paragraph and restates the big idea. This means you use different words to say the same idea. Our paragraph was all about Phoebe being convincing. We need to think of another way of saying this to end our paragraph. A convincing person is persuasive. His or her words sound credible and believable. Here is our conclusion sentence:

Phoebe is such a persuasive person people find her stories credible.

(There is no Step 3 this day, as the modeling leads directly to independent work.)

STEP 4 • Practice through independent work.

Betsy: Your job now is to write your own conclusion sentence. Remember, write the same idea that is in your topic sentence but use different words.

(Betsy walks around and supports students as they work. Then she displays the completed organizer for the class example.)

Analytical Paragraph Organizer Exemplar

COMPONENTS	YOU TRY IT
Topic Sentence: What inference am I trying to prove in this paragraph?	Phoebe, Sal's friend from *Walk Two Moons* by Sharon Creech, is a very convincing person.
A sentence that answers this question: **What more can I say** about the inference in my topic sentence?	She is able to get Sal to believe what she believes and agree with her.
A sentence(s) that answers this question: What **background information** is needed to prepare the reader for the quote in the SmartNote I am using?	Phoebe doesn't trust her neighbor, Mrs. Cadaver, thinking she is a diabolical person.

A **quote**: Which quote best proves the inference from my topic sentence?	She shares her negative opinions with Sal, "'Do you want to know an absolute secret?' Phoebe said. . . . 'Her name is Mrs. Cadaver, right? Have you ever wondered what happened to Mr. Cadaver?'" (p 23).
Sentences that answer this question: How can I **explain/analyze** the quote to show how it proves my inference? This is the So What?	Phoebe is so dramatic she is convincing Sal that something is wrong with Mrs. Cadaver. She raises questions about Mrs. Cadaver that neither one of them can really answer. She convinces Sal to think badly of Mrs. Cadaver just like she does.
Clincher: How can I sum up my thinking?	Phoebe is such a persuasive person that people find her stories credible.

Betsy: Bravo! Job well done. Your organizer is now complete, but this doesn't look like a paragraph yet. A paragraph has all the sentences connected to one another.

(Betsy pulls up the completed paragraph for everyone to view.)

Phoebe, Sal's friend from Walk Two Moons *by Sharon Creech, is a very convincing person. She is able to get Sal to believe what she believes and agree with her. Phoebe doesn't trust her neighbor, Mrs. Cadaver, thinking she is a diabolical person. She shares her negative opinions with Sal, "Do you want to know an absolute secret?' Phoebe said. . . . 'Her name is Mrs. Cadaver, right? Have you ever wondered what happened to Mr. Cadaver?'" (p. 23). Phoebe is so dramatic she is convincing Sal that something is wrong with Mrs. Cadaver. She raises questions about Mrs. Cadaver that neither one of them can really answer. She convinces Sal to think badly of Mrs. Cadaver just like she does. Phoebe is such a persuasive person that people find her stories credible.*

Your job is to now write out your paragraph just like this. Connect each sentence to the next. Do this in your notebook.

Debrief: These mini-lessons required students to use our exemplar and write their own paragraph. To model the process, we used the mentor text. Because students were familiar with this text, we were able to offer more scaffolding during the process. There was a common language and common understanding.

We evaluate students' analytical paragraphs with a rubric (page 117). The rubric uses the same language as the organizer. Using the same terminology eliminates confusion, and students know exactly what is required of them and how to improve their work.

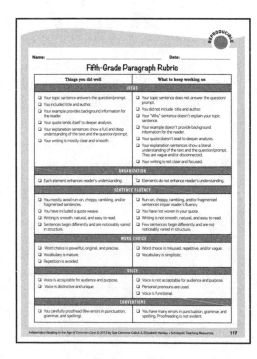

SmartNotes are the heart of an analytical paragraph. Requiring students to use their SmartNotes to push their thinking and prove an idea solidifies the value of SmartNotes. Using SmartNotes to write a formal, structured paragraph is another way to show their importance. Formulating a topic sentence based on SmartNotes, and then proving/supporting that idea with SmartNotes is powerful. This is the kind of thinking and writing about reading that students will need in high school and beyond. Coming up with an organic idea to prove from SmartNotes is the kind of original thinking teachers hope for from their students.

SUGGESTIONS FOR ANALYTICAL PARAGRAPH TOPICS Students' SmartNotes can be used to support any of these topics:

- **Character traits:** Write about the word or words that describe a character's personality.

- **Conflict:** Write about the problems a character struggles with—these can be internal (guilt) or external (nature, society, another person).

- **Conflict:** Write about the problems in a text.

- **Theme/Lesson learned:** Write about theme/central idea in the text. Usually, the theme is determined by looking at how a struggle leads to character change. Theme is often expressed in a single word or phrase, for example: friendship, loyalty, disappointment, loss, love, betrayal, independence, sense of self.

- **Author's message:** Write about how the author's message builds off of the theme. Ask: What is the author saying about the theme? For instance, if the theme is loss, the author could be saying that loss is hard to survive, or maybe that friendships make loss easier to get through.

- **Character change over time:** Write about how the character, like a real person, grows and changes through life.

- **Author's style:** Write about the author's style. Notice the tools the author uses to enhance the reader's understanding or appreciation of the text, including: punctuation, dialogue, short/long sentences, purposeful repetition, word choice, text structure (switch of narration, diary format, letters), literary devices (simile, metaphor, personification, alliteration), foreshadowing, flashback, symbolism.

- **Setting:** Write about the when and where of the story—and its significance for the events and/or character.

USING SMARTNOTES TO LEAD TO A THESIS STATEMENT

An essay is written proof of a student's understanding of and ability to synthesize the big ideas in a text. Students read, analyze, and eventually formulate an idea that they must prove through a multi-paragraph analytical essay. Helping students come up with an idea to prove is where SmartNotes are essential. Students read through their collection of SmartNotes and see evidence of what they have been thinking about through their reading. As we discussed earlier in Chapter 4, students examine their SmartNotes to find threads of thinking. A student may notice many

SmartNotes on character, for example, or perhaps many focused on recurring images. Eventually, these SmartNote-threads are synthesized into a thesis statement. Then the SmartNotes are used to support the thesis idea.

Two pages of SmartNotes from Hallie's notebook are shown at the right. She is reading *From the Mixed-Up Files of Mrs. Basil E. Frankweiler* by E. L. Konigsburg.

When looking over Hallie's SmartNotes, we noticed a lot of great thinking. Her inferences are strong, and she clearly has a good sense of who the characters are. Her thinking is well grounded in the text. As she "smartly" noted on page 18, Claudia and Jaime have a complex relationship. As readers, it is important to notice the way characters interact with one another and change from the experience. During a conference with Hallie, we encouraged her to follow the Jaime/Claudia relationship to notice its ups and downs and how this impacted the plot.

After reading and taking SmartNotes throughout the rest of the text, Hallie was able to create the following thesis statement: *Because Claudia and Jaime have different strengths as individuals, together they make a great team.*

This SmartNote-inspired thesis can be proved. The thinking is Hallie's, and it is proof that she truly understands the text at a deep level. If an essay were required of Hallie, she already has the focus of her essay set with her thesis, and the body paragraphs are ready because she has SmartNotes to support her thesis. Body paragraphs are analytical and follow the same format as the one we shared earlier with *Walk Two Moons*.

With practice and repetition, all readers, all thinkers, are capable of this type of SmartNote synthesis that leads to a thesis. As with the thread/So What? thinking we discussed earlier, you may have to assist students in creating a thesis. You can and should expect this level of accomplishment from all your students.

Conclusion

Middle school is a confusing, electric, and wonderful place where students grow, find themselves, and really blossom. As the year unfolds, your students are not the same readers and thinkers they were when you first met them. We need to support these vibrant learners with a combination of explicit teaching and then letting go. Learning independently, although difficult, is powerful.

You have created a dynamic environment for your students. You have broadened their view of what it means to be a reader. Reading is thinking—and they know this now. Making inferences, asking thoughtful questions, synthesizing information into a thesis—this is the thinking that matters.

Middle school students try to test the limits. This is age appropriate. We need to harness this energy by helping their independence thrive. Picking just-right books—ones in which students are invested, ones they care about—giving them time to think about what is important in the text, and trusting that they can think "smartly" are essential to growing independent, smart middle schoolers. Trusting her students to think was initially hard for Sue (and for all of us, really). But once she did, she grew as a teacher. It revitalized her teaching and was a breath, a change, a revolution of thought. SmartNotes are the perfect instrument; they hold students accountable, yet allow them to be independent at the same time.

In our school and classrooms there is a culture of thinking. Students know they are expected to show their thinking and push the boundaries of thought. Feeling uncomfortable sometimes is okay because thinking is hard. Reading is thinking—and our students live this now. They know they are thinkers. They know they can think through a text and make sense of it. Working through their discomfort results in a sense of accomplishment.

SmartNotes are more than notes. SmartNotes are more than using strategies. SmartNotes are thinking. Something so simple as writing down your thinking as you read altered our curriculum and made it student-focused.

We know our students are great. Every day, they prove this to us through their SmartNotes.

REFERENCES

Allington, R. L. (2009). *What really matters in response to intervention: Research-based designs*. New York: Allyn and Bacon.

Atwell, N. (1998). *In the middle* (2nd ed.). Portsmouth, ME: Boynton/Cook.

Fountas, I., & Pinnell, G. S. (2001). *Guiding readers and writers: Grades 3–6: Teaching comprehension, genre, and content literacy*. Portsmouth, NH: Heinemann.

Fountas, I., & Pinnell, G. S. (2010). *Continuum of literacy learning*. Portsmouth, NH: Heinemann.

Harvey, S., & Goudvis, A. (2000). *Strategies that work*. Portland, ME: Stenhouse.

Robb, L. (2000). *Teaching reading in middle school*. New York: Scholastic.

CHILDREN'S LITERATURE CITED

Appelt, K. (2008). *The underneath*. New York: Simon & Schuster.

Avi. (2001). *The secret school*. New York: Harcourt.

Birdsall, J. (2005). *The Penderwicks: A summer tale of four sisters, two rabbits, and a very interesting boy*. New York: Random House.

Blume, J. (2003). *It's not the end of the world*. New York: Simon & Schuster.

Bosch, P. (2007). *The name of this book is secret*. New York: Hachette.

Brown, J. (2004). *Little cricket*. New York: Hyperion.

Buckley, M. (2009). *NERDS: National Espionage, Rescue, and Defense Society*. New York: Abrams.

Creech, S. (1994). *Walk two moons*. New York: HarperCollins.

Cushman, K. (1994). *Catherine, called Birdy*. New York: Houghton Mifflin Harcourt.

Danziger, P., & Martin, A. M. (1998). *P. S. longer letter later*. New York: Scholastic.

Denenberg, B. (2004). *Atticus of Rome, 30 B.C.* (The life and times series). New York: Scholastic.

Draper, S. (2010). *Out of my mind*. New York: Simon & Schuster.

Edwards, R. (2010). *Who is Barack Obama?* (Who was . . . ? series). New York: Penguin.

Eulberg, E. (2011). *Prom and prejudice*. New York: Scholastic.

Fleischman, S. (2008). *The trouble begins at 8: A life of Mark Twain in the wild, wild west*. New York: HarperCollins.

Fleming, C. (2011). *Amelia lost: The life and disappearance of Amelia Earhart*. New York: Random House.

Fritz, S. (2010). Is corn making us fat? *Junior Scholastic, 112*(11), 4–5.

Gantos, J. (2000). *Joey Pigza loses control*. New York: HarperCollins.

Hinton, S. E. (2012). *The outsiders*. New York: Penguin Group.

Holm, J. L. (2006). *Penny from heaven*. New York: Random House.

Holm, J. L. (2010). *Turtle in paradise*. New York: Random House.

Holt, K. W. (1999). *When Zachary Beaver came to town*. New York: Henry Holt.

Juster, N. (1989). *The phantom tollbooth*. New York: Random House.

Keene, C. (2003). *Nancy Drew: A taste of danger*. New York: Simon & Schuster.

Keene, C. (2004). *Nancy Drew: Action*. New York: Simon & Schuster.

Kinney, J. (2007). *Diary of a wimpy kid, book one*. New York: Abrams.

Kinney, J. (2008). *Diary of a wimpy kid: Rodrick rules*. New York: Abrams.

Koertge, R. (2006). *Shakespeare bats cleanup*. Cambridge, MA: Candlewick.

Konigsburg, E. L. (2007). *From the mixed-up files of Mrs. Basil E. Frankweiler*. New York: Simon & Schuster.

Konigsburg, E. L. (1996). *The view from Saturday*. New York: Simon & Schuster.

Korman, G. (2007). *Schooled*. New York: Hyperion.

Korman, G. (2009). *Zoobreak*. New York: Scholastic.

Kowalski, K. (2009). Let there be light. *Cobblestone, 30*(6), 12–13.

Lewis, C. S.(1978). *The lion, the witch and the wardrobe*. New York: HarperCollins.

Lowry, L. (1989). *Number the stars*. New York: Houghton Mifflin Harcourt.

Lowry, L. (1993). *The giver*. New York: Random House.

Lupica, M. (2010). *Hero.* New York: Penguin.

Marrin, A. (2011). *Flesh and blood so cheap: The Triangle fire and its legacy*. New York: Random House.

Mass, W. (2006). *Jeremy Fink and the meaning of life*. New York: Hachette.

McDonough, Y. Z. (2005). *Who was John F. Kennedy?* New York: Penguin.

Murphy, J. (2003). *An American plague: The true and terrifying story of the yellow fever epidemic of 1793.* New York: Houghton Mifflin.

Murphy, J. (2000). *Blizzard*. New York: Scholastic.

Myers, W. D. (1999). *Monster*. New York: HarperCollins.

Myracle, L. (2009). *Luv Ya Bunches: A flower power book*. New York: Abrams.

Orwell, G. (1973). *Animal farm*. New York: Harcourt Brace.

Paolini, C. (2003). *Eragon*. New York: Random House.

Park, L. S. (2005). *Project mulberry*. New York: Random House.

Paterson, K. (1977). *Bridge to Terabithia*. New York: HarperCollins.

Paulsen, G. (2009). *Hatchet*. New York: Simon & Schuster.

Pearson, R. (2005). *Kingdom keepers: Disney after dark*. New York: Disney.

Philbrick, R. (2001). *Freak the mighty*. New York: Scholastic.

Poltrack, K. (2009). A car for the masses. *Cobblestone, 30*(6), 14–15.

Riggs, R. (2011). *Miss Peregrine's home for peculiar children*. Philadelphia: Quirk.

Riordan, R. (2001). *The lightning thief*. New York: Scholastic.

Rowling, J. K. (2000). *Harry Potter and the goblet of fire*. New York: Scholastic.

Rowling, J. K. (1999). *Harry Potter and the prisoner of Azkaban*. New York: Scholastic.

Ryan, C. (2009). *The forest of hands and teeth*. New York: Random House.

Sachar, L. (1998). *Holes*. New York: Random House.

Schroeder, L. (2010). *It's raining cupcakes*. New York: Simon & Schuster.

Sheinkin, S. (2012). *Bomb: The race to build—and steal—the world's most dangerous weapon*. New York: Roaring Brook Press.

Speare, E. G. (1983). *Sign of the beaver*. New York Houghton Mifflin.

Stewart, T. L. (2007). *The mysterious Benedict Society*. New York: Hachette.

Stiefvater, M. (2011). *The Scorpio races*. New York: Scholastic.

Swanson, J. L. (2009). *Chasing Lincoln's killer*. New York: Scholastic.

Turbow, J., & Duca, M. (2010). *The baseball codes: Beanballs, sign stealing, and bench-clearing brawls: The unwritten rules of America's pastime*. New York: Random House.

Van Draanen. W. (2001). *Flipped*. New York: Knopf.

Van Draanen, W. (2004). *Shredderman: Attack of the tagger*. New York: Random House.

Westerfeld, S. (2009). *Leviathan*. New York: Simon & Schuster Children's Publishing.

White, E. B. (1952). *Charlotte's web*. New York: HarperCollins.

Wiesel, E. (1972). *Night.* New York: Farrar, Straus and Giroux.

Zullo, A. (2006). *Ten true tales: Surviving sharks and other dangerous creatures*. New York: Scholastic.

Book Sign-Out Sheet

DATE OUT	BOOK TITLE AND AUTHOR	STUDENT'S NAME	DATE IN	TEACHER'S INITIALS UPON RETURN

Quick Page Inventory Sheet

STUDENT	TITLE	MON	TUES	WED	THURS	FRI

Name: _____   **Date:** _____

Independent Reading Log

DATE	TITLE AND AUTHOR	PAGE START	PAGE END	PARENT INITIALS

Name: _____   **Date:** _____

SmartNotes Check Sheet

Stop every one or two pages and record your thinking.

Title: _____

QUOTE FROM TEXT AND PAGE NUMBER	MY THINKING

Name: _____ **Date:** _____

SmartNotes Rubric

Page number and quote is included.	0	1		
Writing is legible.	0	1		
Important part of text is reflected upon.	0	1	2	3
Thinking is interesting and clear.	0	1	2	3
A variety of SmartNotes have been tried.	0	1	2	3
So What? is added; student has moved beyond the text.	0	1	2	3

_____ / 14

Weekly Conference Log for the week of _____

MONDAY	TUESDAY	WEDNESDAY	THURSDAY	FRIDAY

Name: _____ **Date:** _____

Literary Letter Assignment

Please follow this outline.

Paragraph 1 What is the title of your book? Who is the author of your book? What is the genre of your book?	
Paragraph 2 What did you think about? Include a quote, your thinking, and a So What?	
Paragraph 3 What did you think about? Include a quote, your thinking, and a So What?	
Paragraph 4 What did you think about? Include a quote, your thinking, and a So What?	
Paragraph 5 Would you recommend this book? Explain why or why not.	

Name: _____   **Date:** _____

Analytical Paragraph Organizer

COMPONENTS	YOU TRY IT
Topic Sentence: What inference am I trying to prove in this paragraph?	
A sentence that answers this question: **What more can I say** about the inference in my topic sentence?	
A sentence(s) that answers this question: What **background information** is needed to prepare the reader for the quote in the SmartNote I am using?	
A quote: Which **quote** best proves the inference from my topic sentence?	
Sentences that answer this question: How can I **explain/analyze** the quote to show how it proves my inference? This is the So What?	
Clincher: How can I sum up my thinking?	

Name: _____   Date: _____

Fifth-Grade Paragraph Rubric

Things you did well	What to keep working on
IDEAS	
❏ Your topic sentence answers the question/prompt. ❏ You included title and author. ❏ Your example provides background information for the reader. ❏ Your quote lends itself to deeper analysis. ❏ Your explanation sentences show a full and deep understanding of the text and the question/prompt. ❏ Your writing is mostly clear and smooth.	❏ Your topic sentence does not answer the question/prompt. ❏ You did not include title and author. ❏ Your "Why" sentence doesn't explain your topic sentence. ❏ Your example doesn't provide background information for the reader. ❏ Your quote doesn't lead to deeper analysis. ❏ Your explanation sentences show a literal understanding of the text and the question/prompt. They are vague and/or disconnected. ❏ Your writing is not clear and focused.
ORGANIZATION	
❏ Each element enhances reader's understanding.	❏ Elements do not enhance reader's understanding.
SENTENCE FLUENCY	
❏ You mostly avoid run-on, choppy, rambling, and/or fragmented sentences. ❏ You have included a quote weave. ❏ Writing is smooth, natural, and easy to read. ❏ Sentences begin differently and are noticeably varied in structure.	❏ Run-on, choppy, rambling, and/or fragmented sentences impair reader's fluency. ❏ You have not woven in your quote. ❏ Writing is not smooth, natural, and easy to read. ❏ Few sentences begin differently and are not noticeably varied in structure.
WORD CHOICE	
❏ Word choice is powerful, original, and precise. ❏ Vocabulary is mature. ❏ Repetition is avoided.	❏ Word choice is misused, repetitive, and/or vague. ❏ Vocabulary is simplistic.
VOICE	
❏ Voice is acceptable for audience and purpose. ❏ Voice is distinctive and unique.	❏ Voice is not acceptable for audience and purpose. ❏ Personal pronouns are used. ❏ Voice is functional.
CONVENTIONS	
❏ You carefully proofread (few errors in punctuation, grammar, and spelling).	❏ You have many errors in punctuation, grammar, and spelling. Proofreading is not evident.

CORRELATION OF SAMPLE MINI-LESSONS TO THE COMMON CORE STATE STANDARDS

Mini-Lesson	CCSS
Summary SmartNotes Mini-Lesson for Fiction, *pages 22–25*	**RL.5.2** Determine a theme of a story, drama, or poem from details in the text, including how characters in a story or drama respond to challenges or how the speaker in a poem reflects upon a topic; summarize the text. **RL.6.2** Determine a theme or central idea of a text and how it is conveyed through particular details; provide a summary of the text distinct from personal opinions or judgments. **RL.7.2** Determine a theme or central idea of a text and analyze its development over the course of the text; provide an objective summary of the text. **RL.8.2** Determine a theme or central idea of a text and analyze its development over the course of the text, including its relationship to the characters, setting, and plot; provide an objective summary of the text.
Determining Importance SmartNotes Mini-Lesson for Fiction, *pages 25–27*	**RL.5.1** Quote accurately from a text when explaining what the text says explicitly and when drawing inferences from the text. **RL.5.2** Determine a theme of a story, drama, or poem from details in the text, including how characters in a story or drama respond to challenges or how the speaker in a poem reflects upon a topic; summarize the text. **RL.6.1** Cite textual evidence to support analysis of what the text says explicitly as well as inferences drawn from the text. **RL.6.2** Determine a theme or central idea of a text and how it is conveyed through particular details; provide a summary of the text distinct from personal opinions or judgments. **RL.7.1** Cite several pieces of textual evidence to support analysis of what the text says explicitly as well as inferences drawn from the text. **RL.7.2** Determine a theme or central idea of a text and analyze its development over the course of the text; provide an objective summary of the text. **RL.8.1** Cite the textual evidence that most strongly supports an analysis of what the text says explicitly as well as inferences drawn from the text. **RL.8.2** Determine a theme or central idea of a text and analyze its development over the course of the text, including its relationship to the characters, setting, and plot; provide an objective summary of the text.

Mini-Lesson	CCSS
Determining Importance SmartNotes Mini-Lesson for Nonfiction, *pages 28–30*	**RI.5.1** Quote accurately from a text when explaining what the text says explicitly and when drawing inferences from the text. **RI.5.2** Determine two or more main ideas of a text and explain how they are supported by key details; summarize the text. **RI.6.1** Cite textual evidence to support analysis of what the text says explicitly as well as inferences drawn from the text. **RI.6.2** Determine a central idea of a text and how it is conveyed through particular details; provide a summary of the text distinct from personal opinions or judgments. **RI.7.1** Cite several pieces of textual evidence to support analysis of what the text says explicitly as well as inferences drawn from the text. **RI.7.2** Determine a theme or central idea of a text and analyze its development over the course of the text; provide an objective summary of the text. **RI.8.1** Cite the textual evidence that most strongly supports an analysis of what the text says explicitly as well as inferences drawn from the text. **RI.8.2** Determine a theme or central idea of a text and analyze its development over the course of the text, including its relationship to the characters, setting, and plot; provide an objective summary of the text.
Using Text Features SmartNotes Mini-Lesson for Nonfiction, *pages 30–32*	**RI.5.5** Compare and contrast the overall structure (e.g., chronology, comparison, cause/effect, problem/solution) of events, ideas, concepts, or information in two or more texts. **RI.6.5** Analyze how a particular sentence, paragraph, chapter, or section fits into the overall structure of a text and contributes to the development of the ideas. **RI.7.5** Analyze the structure an author uses to organize a text, including how the major sections contribute to the whole and to the development of the ideas. **RI.8.5** Analyze in detail the structure of a specific paragraph in a text, including the role of particular sentences in developing and refining a key concept.

Mini-Lesson	CCSS
Text-to-Self Connections SmartNotes Mini-Lesson for Fiction, *pages 32–34*	**RL.5.1** Quote accurately from a text when explaining what the text says explicitly and when drawing inferences from the text. **RL.5.3** Compare and contrast two or more characters, settings, or events in a story or drama, drawing on specific details in the text (e.g., how characters interact). **RL.6.1** Cite textual evidence to support analysis of what the text says explicitly as well as inferences drawn from the text. **RL.6.3** Describe how a particular story's or drama's plot unfolds in a series of episodes as well as how the characters respond or change as the plot moves toward a resolution. **RL.7.1** Cite several pieces of textual evidence to support analysis of what the text says explicitly as well as inferences drawn from the text. **RL.7.3** Analyze how particular elements of a story or drama interact (e.g., how setting shapes the characters or plot). **RL.8.1** Cite the textual evidence that most strongly supports an analysis of what the text says explicitly as well as inferences drawn from the text. **RL.8.3** Analyze how particular lines of dialogue or incidents in a story or drama propel the action, reveal aspects of a character, or provoke a decision.
Visualizing SmartNotes Mini-Lesson for Fiction, *pages 35–37*	**RL.5.4** Determine the meaning of words and phrases as they are used in a text, including figurative language such as metaphors and similes. **RL.6.4** Determine the meaning of words and phrases as they are used in a text, including figurative and connotative meanings; analyze the impact of a specific word choice on meaning and tone. **RL.7.4** Determine the meaning of words and phrases as they are used in a text, including figurative and connotative meanings; analyze the impact of rhymes and other repetitions of sounds (e.g., alliteration) on a specific verse or stanza of a poem or section of a story or drama. **RL.8.4** Determine the meaning of words and phrases as they are used in a text, including figurative and connotative meanings; analyze the impact of specific word choices on meaning and tone, including analogies or allusions to other texts.

Mini-Lesson	CCSS
Visualizing SmartNotes Mini-Lesson for Nonfiction, *pages 37–39*	**RI.5.4** Determine the meaning of general academic and domain-specific words and phrases in a text relevant to a *grade 5 topic or subject area.*
	RI.5.5 Compare and contrast the overall structure (e.g., chronology, comparison, cause/effect, problem/solution) of events, ideas, concepts, or information in two or more texts.
	RI.6.4 Determine the meaning of words and phrases as they are used in a text, including figurative, connotative, and technical meanings.
	RI.6.5 Analyze how a particular sentence, paragraph, chapter, or section fits into the overall structure of a text and contributes to the development of the ideas.
	RI.7.4 Determine the meaning of words and phrases as they are used in a text, including figurative, connotative, and technical meanings; analyze the impact of a specific word choice on meaning and tone.
	RI.7.5 Analyze the structure an author uses to organize a text, including how the major sections contribute to the whole and to the development of the ideas.
	RI.8.4 Determine the meaning of words and phrases as they are used in a text, including figurative, connotative, and technical meanings; analyze the impact of specific word choices on meaning and tone, including analogies or allusions to other texts.
	RI.8.5 Analyze in detail the structure of a specific paragraph in a text, including the role of particular sentences in developing and refining a key concept.

Mini-Lesson	CCSS
Questioning SmartNotes Mini-Lesson for Fiction, *pages 40–42*	**RL.5.5** Explain how a series of chapters, scenes, or stanzas fits together to provide the overall structure of a particular story, drama, or poem.
	RL.5.6 Describe how a narrator's or speaker's point of view influences how events are described.
	RL.6.5 Analyze how a particular sentence, chapter, scene, or stanza fits into the overall structure of a text and contributes to the development of the theme, setting, or plot.
	RL.6.6 Explain how an author develops the point of view of the narrator or speaker in a text.
	RL.7.5 Analyze how a drama's or poem's form or structure (e.g., soliloquy, sonnet) contributes to its meaning.
	RL.7.6 Analyze how an author develops and contrasts the points of view of different characters or narrators in a text.
	RL.8.5 Compare and contrast the structure of two or more texts and analyze how the differing structure of each text contributes to its meaning and style.
	RL.8.6 Analyze how differences in the points of view of the characters and the audience or reader (e.g., created through the use of dramatic irony) create such effects as suspense or humor.

Mini-Lesson	CCSS
Clarifying Confusion SmartNote Mini-Lesson for Nonfiction, *pages 43–44*	**RI.5.4** Determine the meaning of general academic and domain-specific words and phrases in a text relevant to a *grade 5 topic or subject area*.
	RI.6.4 Determine the meaning of words and phrases as they are used in a text, including figurative, connotative, and technical meanings.
	RI.7.4 Determine the meaning of words and phrases as they are used in a text, including figurative, connotative, and technical meanings; analyze the impact of a specific word choice on meaning and tone.
	RI.8.4 Determine the meaning of words and phrases as they are used in a text, including figurative, connotative, and technical meanings; analyze the impact of specific word choices on meaning and tone, including analogies or allusions to other texts.
	L.5.4 Determine or clarify the meaning of unknown and multiple-meaning words and phrases based on grade 5 reading and content, choosing flexibly from a range of strategies.
	L.6.4 Use context (e.g., the overall meaning of a sentence or paragraph; a word's position or function in a sentence) as a clue to the meaning of a word or phrase.
	L.7.4 Determine or clarify the meaning of unknown and multiple-meaning words and phrases based on *grade 7 reading and content*, choosing flexibly from a range of strategies.
	L.8.4 Determine or clarify the meaning of unknown and multiple-meaning words or phrases based on *grade 8 reading and content*, choosing flexibly from a range of strategies.

Mini-Lesson	CCSS
Predicting SmartNotes Mini-Lesson for Fiction, *pages 45–47*	**RL.5.3** Compare and contrast two or more characters, settings, or events in a story or drama, drawing on specific details in the text (e.g., how characters interact). **RL.5.5** Compare and contrast two or more characters, settings, or events in a story or drama, drawing on specific details in the text (e.g., how characters interact). **RL.6.3** Describe how a particular story's or drama's plot unfolds in a series of episodes as well as how the characters respond or change as the plot moves toward a resolution. **RL.6.5** Analyze how a particular sentence, chapter, scene, or stanza fits into the overall structure of a text and contributes to the development of the theme, setting, or plot. **RL.7.3** Analyze how particular elements of a story or drama interact (e.g., how setting shapes the characters or plot). **RL.7.5** Analyze how a drama's or poem's form or structure (e.g., soliloquy, sonnet) contributes to its meaning. **RL.8.3** Analyze how particular lines of dialogue or incidents in a story or drama propel the action, reveal aspects of a character, or provoke a decision. **RL.8.5** Compare and contrast the structure of two or more texts and analyze how the differing structure of each text contributes to its meaning and style.
Text-to-Text Connections SmartNotes Mini-Lesson for Fiction, *pages 47–50*	**RL.5.9** Compare and contrast stories in the same genre (e.g., mysteries and adventure stories) on their approaches to similar themes and topics. **RL.6.9** Compare and contrast texts in different forms or genres (e.g., stories and poems; historical novels and fantasy stories) in terms of their approaches to similar themes and topics. **RL.7.9** Compare and contrast a fictional portrayal of a time, place, or character and a historical account of the same period as a means of understanding how authors of fiction use or alter history. **RL.8.9** Analyze how a modern work of fiction draws on themes, patterns of events, or character types from myths, traditional stories, or religious works such as the Bible, including describing how the material is rendered new.

Mini-Lesson	CCSS
Text-to-World Connections SmartNotes Mini-Lesson for Fiction, *pages 50–52*	**RL.5.6** Describe how a narrator's or speaker's point of view influences how events are described. **RL.6.6** Explain how an author develops the point of view of the narrator or speaker in a text. **RL.7.6** Analyze how an author develops and contrasts the points of view of different characters or narrators in a text. **RL.8.6** Analyze how differences in the points of view of the characters and the audience or reader (e.g., created through the use of dramatic irony) create such effects as suspense or humor.
Inferring SmartNotes Mini-Lesson for Fiction, *pages 52–55*	**RL.5.1** Quote accurately from a text when explaining what the text says explicitly and when drawing inferences from the text. **RL.6.1** Cite textual evidence to support analysis of what the text says explicitly as well as inferences drawn from the text. **RL.7.1** Cite several pieces of textual evidence to support analysis of what the text says explicitly as well as inferences drawn from the text. **RL.8.1** Cite the textual evidence that most strongly supports an analysis of what the text says explicitly as well as inferences drawn from the text.
Synthesizing SmartNotes Mini-Lesson for Nonfiction, *pages 56–58*	**RI.5.8** Explain how an author uses reasons and evidence to support particular points in a text, identifying which reasons and evidence support which point(s). **RI.6.8** Trace and evaluate the argument and specific claims in a text, distinguishing claims that are supported by reasons and evidence from claims that are not. **RI.7.8** Trace and evaluate the argument and specific claims in a text, assessing whether the reasoning is sound and the evidence is relevant and sufficient to support the claims. **RI.8.8** Delineate and evaluate the argument and specific claims in a text, assessing whether the reasoning is sound and the evidence is relevant and sufficient; recognize when irrelevant evidence is introduced.

Mini-Lesson	CCSS
Close Reading Protocol, *pages 62–64*	**RI.5.2** Determine two or more main ideas of a text and explain how they are supported by key details; summarize the text.
	RI.5.3 Explain the relationships or interactions between two or more individuals, events, ideas, or concepts in a historical, scientific, or technical text based on specific information in the text.
	RI.5.8 Explain how an author uses reasons and evidence to support particular points in a text, identifying which reasons and evidence support which point(s).
	RI.6.2 Determine a central idea of a text and how it is conveyed through particular details; provide a summary of the text distinct from personal opinions or judgments.
	RI.6.3 Analyze in detail how a key individual, event, or idea is introduced, illustrated, and elaborated in a text (e.g., through examples or anecdotes).
	RI.6.8 Trace and evaluate the argument and specific claims in a text, distinguishing claims that are supported by reasons and evidence from claims that are not.
	RI.7.2 Determine two or more central ideas in a text and analyze their development over the course of the text; provide an objective summary of the text.
	RI.7.3 Analyze the interactions between individuals, events, and ideas in a text (e.g., how ideas influence individuals or events, or how individuals influence ideas or events).
	RI.7.8 Trace and evaluate the argument and specific claims in a text, assessing whether the reasoning is sound and the evidence is relevant and sufficient to support the claims.
	RI.8.2 Determine a central idea of a text and analyze its development over the course of the text, including its relationship to supporting ideas; provide an objective summary of the text.
	RI.8.3 Analyze how a text makes connections among and distinctions between individuals, ideas, or events (e.g., through comparisons, analogies, or categories).
	RI.8.8 Delineate and evaluate the argument and specific claims in a text, assessing whether the reasoning is sound and the evidence is relevant and sufficient; recognize when irrelevant evidence is introduced.

Mini-Lesson	CCSS
About-the-Text Thinking SmartNotes Mini-Lesson, *pages 91–93*	**RI.5.5** Compare and contrast the overall structure (e.g., chronology, comparison, cause/effect, problem/solution) of events, ideas, concepts, or information in two or more texts. **RI.6.5** Analyze how a particular sentence, paragraph, chapter, or section fits into the overall structure of a text and contributes to the development of the ideas. **RI.7.5** Analyze the structure an author uses to organize a text, including how the major sections contribute to the whole and to the development of the ideas. **RI.8.5** Analyze in detail the structure of a specific paragraph in a text, including the role of particular sentences in developing and refining a key concept.

Mini-Lesson	CCSS
Character Trait Analytical Paragraph SmartNote Mini-Lesson, *pages 97–103*	**W.5.1** Write opinion pieces on topics or texts, supporting a point of view with reasons and information. **W.5.2** Write informative/explanatory texts to examine a topic and convey ideas and information clearly. **W.5.8** Recall relevant information from experiences or gather relevant information from print and digital sources; summarize or paraphrase information in notes and finished work, and provide a list of sources. **W.6.1** Write arguments to support claims with clear reasons and relevant evidence. **W.6.2** Write informative/explanatory texts to examine a topic and convey ideas, concepts, and information through the selection, organization, and analysis of relevant content. **W.6.8** Gather relevant information from multiple print and digital sources; assess the credibility of each source; and quote or paraphrase the data and conclusions of others while avoiding plagiarism and providing basic bibliographic information for sources. **W.7.1** Write arguments to support claims with clear reasons and relevant evidence. **W.7.2** Write informative/explanatory texts to examine a topic and convey ideas, concepts, and information through the selection, organization, and analysis of relevant content. **W.7.8** Gather relevant information from multiple print and digital sources, using search terms effectively; assess the credibility and accuracy of each source; and quote or paraphrase the data and conclusions of others while avoiding plagiarism and following a standard format for citation. **W.8.1** Write arguments to support claims with clear reasons and relevant evidence. **W.8.2** Write informative/explanatory texts to examine a topic and convey ideas, concepts, and information through the selection, organization, and analysis of relevant content. **W.8.8** Gather relevant information from multiple print and digital sources, using search terms effectively; assess the credibility and accuracy of each source; and quote or paraphrase the data and conclusions of others while avoiding plagiarism and following a standard format for citation.